D0848787

The Need for Interpretation

The Need for Interpretation

CONTEMPORARY CONCEPTIONS OF THE PHILOSOPHER'S TASK

edited by

Sollace Mitchell and Michael Rosen

THE ATHLONE PRESS · LONDON
HUMANITIES PRESS · NEW JERSEY

First published 1983, in Great Britain by
The Athlone Press Ltd, 58 Russell Square,
London WC1B 4HL, and in the USA by
Humanities Press Inc, New Jersey.

© The Athlone Press Ltd 1983

British Library Cataloguing in Publication Data
The need for interpretation: contemporary
conceptions of the philosopher's task.
1. Analysis (Philosophy) — Addresses, essays,
lectures   2. Philosophy, Modern — 20th century
— Addresses, essays, lectures
I. Mitchell, Sollace   II. Rosen, Michael
190   B808.5

UK SBN 0-485-11224-8
USA SBN 0-391-02825-1

Typeset in Plantin by Inforum Ltd, Portsmouth
Printed in Great Britain by
Nene Litho, Earls Barton, Northants
Bound by Woolnough Bookbinding, Wellingborough, Northants

Contents

Preface

The essays in this book originated in a nagging dissatisfaction with analytical philosophy as it has recently been practised in England and America. Each of the contributors has studied or taught in the faculty of philosophy at Oxford University, a bastion of the analytical movement if anything is. A shared antipathy towards the doctrines prevailing there is what first drew us together and led to the formation of a weekly discussion group.

Among Oxford philosophers there are many such alliances, born of expediency, perhaps in our case, desperation, most of which are named for the day on which they meet. The name of our particular cell, The Friday Afternoon (and later on, Morning) Discussion Group, doubtless never sufficiently distinguished us from the innumerable conclaves of the less disaffected. What surely did set us apart was our suspicion that there was more to life than realism, anti-realism, empiricism, or idealism. One quickly learns that induction into the world of professional philosophy is tantamount to being 'ismed' into stupefaction.

We assume we are not unique in our discontent with the received alternatives in Anglo-American philosophy. What was notable about the Friday afternoon group, however, was that over the course of its three-year life we were unable to reach any consensus about just what analytical philosophy is. There seems to be no single characteristic that would identify it in the hands of those philosophers commonly acknowledged as its leading practitioners. Yet, even though we could not pin down analytical philosophy, we remained convinced that it left something to be desired. Furthermore, though we complained against the dogmas of the tradition, we were acutely aware that we wrote from within it and that our style of inquiry, even our prejudices, were informed (though not dominated) by the popular tendencies toward formalism and natural scientific empiricism.

If we were able to resist subscribing to the more patently biased dogmas, it is because we were to varying degrees familiar with a competing view of the philosophical enterprise, one often called the '*verstehen*' approach and associated with German and French philosophers of the past hundred years. To characterize continental philosophy as embodying an 'understanding' approach is not to charge Anglo-American philosophy with seeking no understanding; but the aims of the two traditions are different. Whereas the latter might be said to want an explanation of human behaviour that would be reducible to or convergent with natural science, the former may be said to want an interpretation of human discourse that illuminates the subject in the context of his social practices.

An awareness of the tension between these two views unites the papers that follow. The briefest possible description of the common position taken by the contributors would be that they embrace the methods but not the aims of analytical philosophy, and the aims but not the methods of continental philosophy. It is the editors' hope that this cryptic statement will come clear in reading the introduction and essays that comprise several contemporary conceptions of the philosopher's task.

The six contributors represent only a part of those who participated in the Friday afternoon group. The editors would therefore like to thank the following people who argued with and against us and, in so doing, contributed as much as any of us to what is contained in this book: Josef Buscher, Corby Collins, Daniel Dennett, Kurt Hilgenburg, Steve Holtzman, Chris Janaway, Alan Montefiore and Galen Strawson. We should also like to thank Ms Linda Zuck, who received the idea for this book enthusiastically and helped to ensure that it would, eventually, get published.

Introduction

That current Anglo-American philosophy should lack an agreed conception of the philosopher's task is not, by historical standards, unusual. Nor need it be taken as an indicator of debility. To the contrary, much great philosophy was developed in the ferment of dispute with received conceptions of the discipline. What is open to criticism is not the lack of an agreed conception so much as the fact that such broad issues now receive so little reflection.

There are several reasons for this. One has to do with a tendency, especially marked in America, to turn philosophy into a simulacrum of the natural sciences. Although it is unable to match them in their contribution to technical progress much recent philosophy has imitated the sciences' abstractness and formality – perhaps in the hope of sharing their prestige. In these circumstances general discussions of the scope and methods of philosophy are unwelcome, a distraction from 'scientific business'.

British philosophers, on the other hand, have been less keen to borrow status from the sciences – perhaps, in Britain, there has been less of it to borrow. But nor have they shown any great inclination to raise general questions of approach. There is a fear that such discussions are inevitably insubstantial. The prevailing ethos is one of 'getting on with the job'. To British philosophers the reflexive preoccupations of continental philosophy appear narcissistic, redolent of that unhealthy self-absorption which the British have always distrusted in foreigners.

This neglect of general questions of method is magnified by analytical philosophy's reluctance to situate itself historically; or, when it does so, to adopt a very selective view of philosophical history. In turning its attention to the past analytical philosophy has concentrated, for the most part, on its differences with British Empiricism and this has given its image of philosophical development an inappropriately rigid perspective. It is as if the alternatives – analytical philosophy or empiricism – set the limits to the ultimate dimensions of philosophy's problems. More discriminating attempts to relate philosophy to its historical and social contexts are seen as threats to detach philosophy from its concern with truth and dissolve it into the history of ideas.

These are, it must be said, only tendencies. For, of course, some conception of the broad course of philosophical history is inseparable from the practice of the discipline. Nevertheless such conceptions are frequently inarticulate and crude. We would point to three current examples.

The first is the view that analytical philosophy can be identified by adherence to novel common doctrines which distinguish it from the philosophy of the past. The objection to this view is that the only two obvious candidates for such a role by no means command universal adherence. Neither the doctrine of logical form (the idea that the methods of logic developed by Frege and his successors have disclosed the true structure of language) nor verificationism (the commitment to the test of verifiability as a means, as Ayer puts it, 'to delineate the conditions under which alone a sentence can be literally significant') have stood the test of time. Indeed, it is hard to think of a single contemporary author who would adopt either label without reservation.

A second view is that analytical philosophy can be identified, not by common doctrines, but by the character of its approach to problems. The barriers between traditions are differences of style rather than substance: the precise and argumentative versus the speculative and rhetorical. Continental philosophers, not surprisingly, find this characterization cavalier and superficial. At its most vulgar it assumes that non-analytical philosophers are simply not serious – and therefore not worth serious study. At this level there is, of course, no reply.

A third conception of analytical philosophy is more widespread outside the tradition itself. This conception takes analytical philosophy to be no more than a revival of some earlier approach, or approaches. Marxist writers are particularly inclined to make this judgement. Committed to the belief that the central issues of philosophy have been definitively resolved (or superseded) by the work of Marx and Engels, Marxist philosophers have strong reasons to deny that philosophy might still be capable of radically new development.

Analytical philosophy is thus taken to be a species of *empiricism* (the doctrine that only what has been given to us in sense experience can play a substantive role in our knowledge of the world); of *positivism* (the belief that the natural sciences offer a privileged model of rationality); or of *formalism* (the belief – connected to positivism – that only such material as can be represented in the notation of logic or mathematics is truly cognitive). Certainly, elements of all three doctrines are present in analytical philosophy. None of them, however, is unchallenged. No single philosopher has had more influence on contemporary analytical philosophy than the later Wittgenstein, and yet he is vigorously opposed to all three tendencies.

We believe it is possible to see two great streams of thought about the nature of the philosopher's task running through the history of Western philosophy. Positivism, formalism and (with some qualification) empiricism are aspects of one of these streams. But it is a stream which goes back much further than any of these doctrines – certainly to the Greeks. For this reason we shall refer to it under a more inclusive name: the *enlightenment* conception of philosophy.

The enlightenment conception views philosophy in the context of humanity's transition from a mythical to a secular world-view – the passage from *mythos* to *logos*. Rational, secular knowledge is epitomized in the natural sciences and so, for the enlightenment philosopher, philosophy must be cognate with the sciences. Either it is to become a branch of science itself (the science of thought, perhaps) or to function as a propadeutic to science, preparing the conceptual ground where the edifice of science is to be constructed.

But there is another traditional conception of the philosopher's task and this, too, has been represented (although less prominently) in the analytical tradition. This conception does not restrict philosophy to the role of 'underlabourer' to the natural sciences, but assesses it more broadly, in terms of the contribution it makes to human understanding in general – to our ability to find the world and our deeds in it intelligible. We may call this the *understanding* conception of philosophy.

Are these two aspirations necessarily in conflict with one another? They have not always been thought to be. Both were at work together in Greek philosophy in the concept of *theoria*:

The word 'theory' has religious origins. The *theoros* was the representative sent by Greek cities to public celebrations. Through *theoria*, that is through looking on, he abandoned himself to the sacred events. In philosophical language, *theoria* was transferred to contemplation of the cosmos. . . . When the philosopher views the immortal order, he cannot help bringing himself into accord with the proportions of the cosmos and reproducing them internally. He manifests these proportions, which he sees in the motions of nature and the harmonic series of music, within himself; he forms himself through mimesis. Through the soul's likening itself to the ordered motion of the cosmos, theory enters the conduct of life. In *ethos* theory moulds life to its form and is reflected in the conduct of those who subject themselves to its discipline.

(J. Habermas, *Knowledge and Human Interests*, pp. 301–2)

But since then, as Habermas recognizes, the two streams have become detached from one another. Hegel's 'philosophical theodicy', his attempt to integrate the most comprehensive scientific knowledge in the service of the formation (the *Bildung*) and reconciliation of the individual, turns out to have been a high-water mark of philosophical ambition. More recent philosophy seems, rather, to confirm Max Weber's judgement that a loss of the ability to see the world as intrinsically meaningful is part of the price to be paid for the progress of rationality.

On the face of it this conflict between meaning and rational knowledge seems to support an enlightenment approach to philosophy. One can imagine the following argument. Let us admit, the defender of the enlightenment conception might say, that there is a price to be paid for the progress of rationality. Yet what is being lost is not something which, properly, forms part of philosophy. Philosophy, if it is anything, is rational and discursive. But what must be given up – our ability to see the world as part of a meaningful cosmos – is at best something pseudo-rational, the emotions masquerading as the intellect. As men and women (we can hear the voices of Hume, Mill and Russell) we must not commit the intellectualist fallacy that what is not rational is not personally or socially valuable; but let us leave poetry to the poets.

To this argument there are two important kinds of response. The first, relatively moderate in its implications for the enlightenment conception, amounts to the claim that philosophy includes in its subject matter material which cannot be treated as the object of a scientific theory. The second response is more radical. It does not identify an area neglected by the enlightenment conception; it attacks the enlightenment conception of rationality itself. In its most extreme version – held, for example, by Nietzsche and his followers – the claim is that the enlightenment ideal of science is itself a myth (a myth, the philosophers of the Frankfurt School add, which legitimates a technocratically ordered society).

The first type of argument can be seen at work in the view of analytical philosophy described by Richard Hare as 'a demythologised version of Plato's doctrine of anamnesis' (R. Hare, 'Philosophical Discoveries', p. 208). The characterization is appropriate. Philosophy for Plato – as also for Hare and those who agree with him – recalls to us what we already know. In this sense philosophy is a form of self-understanding rather than a branch of science. But for analytical philosophers what is to be recalled is not an object, once known but now submerged, as it were, beneath the waters of consciousness. It is a practice unreflectively engaged in – a 'knowing how' in Gilbert Ryle's phrase – that philosophy is to convert to an explicit 'knowing that'.

Hare is defending a classic version of 'ordinary language philosophy', the school which dominated at Oxford in the fifties and sixties. Its claim that the task of philosophy is to undertake such anamnetic analysis rests on two crucial assumptions. The first is the assumption that to speak a language is to engage in a systematic social practice, governed by rules. Although we may not be explicitly aware of them, it is these rules which regulate the activity and underpin our ability to communicate with one another. They function as a standard for the practice. They function, too, as the ideal for the practice of philosophical analysis, in the way that the ideal of a logically perfect language did at an earlier stage in analytical philosophy's development.

Ordinary language philosophy's second crucial assumption is connected to this: that philosophy is concerned with conceptual, not empirical issues (which, of course, presupposes, in turn, that it is possible to separate the two). If this assumption holds, it should be possible to decide philosophical issues – the dispute between free will and determinism, and so on – without the need to wait for outstanding questions of scientific fact to be settled.

Ordinary language philosophy was bitterly opposed from its inception. But many of the early attacks on it were not directed at these two fundamental assumptions. It was alleged, for example, that ordinary language philosophy was trivial, that it treated issues of substance as if they were solely issues about the use of words. Sophisticated ordinary language philosophers had, however, a strong reply available to such objections: so far from dissolving substantive issues, linguistic analysis strengthens our capacity to address them. As J.L. Austin says, 'we are looking . . . not *merely* at words . . . but also at the realities we use words to talk about: we are using a sharpened awareness of words to sharpen our perception of, though not as the final arbiter of, the phenomena' ('A Plea for Excuses', p. 130).

More recently, however, objection has indeed focused on these two central assumptions. The most influential have come from America where they have been associated with the names of Quine and Davidson in particular. Quine has attacked the analytic–synthetic distinction (the distinction between those sentences which are true, if they are at all, in virtue of the meanings of their terms, and those which require external evidence). In so doing he calls into question the basis for ordinary language philosophy's required distinction between conceptual and empirical issues. Davidson, in his turn, has attempted to show that it is possible to construct a systematic account of language which does not treat rule-governedness as a primitive assumption: 'Just as *Lear* gains in power through the absence of Cordelia, I think treatments of language prosper when they avoid uncritical evocation of the concepts of convention, linguistic rule, linguistic practice, or language games' ('Reply to Foster', p. 33).

Quine's and Davidson's are counter-attacks from within the enlightenment stream of analytical philosophy. Thus they draw attention to the more radical response to the enlightenment approach to philosophy.

For the enlightenment view of philosophy as cognate with the natural sciences to have content it is necessary to be able to identify those features of science which constitute its scientific status. But this, it is charged, is just what the development of modern science has shown that the enlightenment conception of philosophy fails to do.

In the heyday of the Enlightenment itself there was a general belief that it was possible to identify true science by a combination of the form of explanation used and the domain of objects dealt with. Kant is a good example. In his vision of things the scientist (modelled on Newton) discovers the deductively connected system of empirical laws governing the motion of bodies in space and time. Scientists describe the universe solely in terms of the causal relations of matter in motion. All is open to observation, its coherence and closure guaranteed by *a priori* reasoning.

Even Kant was troubled by the possibility that there might be other sciences (biology, for example) which do not have this classic form. Such sciences were not, he said, as yet fully scientific and could not share in the closure and rigour of 'pure science of nature'.

But developments since Kant have made the simple identification of science with the Newtonian world-view untenable. Indeed, scientists after Einstein have had to come to terms with the idea that no single vision of the order of nature will identify science once and for all: development may repeatedly force us to revise our ontologies (our view of what there, ultimately, is).

This leaves a dilemma for the scientifically-oriented philosopher, however. For the form of scientific explanation (the deductively connected structure of laws) alone appears to be insufficient to function as the criterion of rationality that the enlightenment approach needs. It has been argued that this deductive-nomological form neither characterizes science exhaustively (the sciences also contain material in other forms) nor exclusively (other non-scientific disciplines also construct law-statements).

Thus enlightenment philosophers have looked to replace the association of science with a unique ontology by a specifically scientific methodology. If the ontology of science had been taken to represent the ultimate structure of reality, the justification of method involves reference to the goals of investigation. This, however, invites the challenge that goals appropriate to natural science – maximizing control of nature, for example – cannot be taken to be universal features of rationality. There may be other fields – social life, above all – in which these goals are inappropriate. Philosophers such as Richard Bernstein, Jürgen Habermas, Richard Rorty, and – in this collection – David Kirsh, have argued that the instrumentalist turn in the philosophy of science prepares the ground for a critique of scientific reason.

It is not clear to what extent such conflicts undermine analytical philosophy. It is true that they challenge two dominant trends – ordinary language philosophy and positivism. Nevertheless, analytical philosophy cannot necessarily be reduced to (and thus dismissed with) these trends. Furthermore, a simple transfer of allegiance from analytical to continental philosophy may not be a solution. If the arguments given by the editors in their contributions are sound, it would appear that contemporary German and French alternatives rest on assumptions as dubious as those of the positivist philosophies they oppose. Although they are by no means unanimous in the conclusions which they draw, all the contributors to this volume are conscious of these challenges.

This is why the later philosophy of Wittgenstein assumes a central role in the collection. In intention, at least, Wittgenstein's work incorporates a resolution of these dilemmas. He aims to skirt traditional philosophy's objectionable 'isms' – materialism, idealism, positivism, empiricism, etc. Most importantly, he also takes to heart the three developments present in the analytical tradition which, in our opinion, no contemporary philosophy – whether advancing the enlightenment or understanding conception of the philosopher's task – can ignore.

These developments point towards an answer to the question of analytical philosophy's identity. Although they are distinguishing features they are, crucially, not positive common doctrines like the doctrine of logical form or verificationism. They should be seen, rather, as conditions governing the terrain on which conceptions of the philosopher's task now compete. The three developments are: (1) a rejection of the idea that the structure of language may be unproblematically read off from its surface grammatical form; (2) an awareness of the difficulty now facing any attempt to give an account of what is essential to science; (3) the rejection of psychologism.

To take them in turn:

(1) It is well known that Wittgenstein's later views on the structure of language amount to a rejection of his own earlier adherence to the doctrine of logical form. But it should also be appreciated that they are not simply a return to traditional views. In the *Tractatus* he wrote that 'Russell's merit is to have shown that the apparent logical form of a proposition need not be its real form' (*Tractatus Logico-Philosophicus* 4.0031). It is a statement which his later self could quite well have

echoed. He would have disputed, however, his earlier corollary: the claim that the real form had now, finally, been disclosed. Although in his later writings Wittgenstein continues to challenge the view that the 'depth grammar' of language mirrors its surface structure, he is at pains to deny that this depth grammar is itself the unique essential skeleton of language. Structures are only identified relative to language-games, and these language-games are multiform.

(2) The idea of language-games is also used to support a resolutely anti-essentialist view of the status of different sciences. The stress on the diversity of language-games emphasizes that, in Wittgenstein's view, there is no single identifying structure common to all sciences. It has meant that Wittgenstein has often been labelled an epistemological nihilist, sceptical of any attempt to assess the validity of cognitive practices. If this serious charge is to be deflected then (as Christopher Leich and Theodore Schatzki's discussions make clear) the Wittgensteinian must show how standards are developed within the course of the individual practices themselves.

(3) Anti-psychologism is significantly ambiguous: it expresses the (quite different) ideas that philosophical issues can be dealt with without reference to the nature of mental life, and that mental life has been misconceived as the intrinsically private contents of an individual psyche.

The first conception of anti-psychologism came to the fore with Frege's distinction between *Sinn* (meaning – the proper, public object of philosophical concern) and *Vorstellung* (the private mental image with which it is associated). Michael Dummett takes this to be the key to Frege's significance in the history of philosophy:

> Only with Frege was the proper object of philosophy finally established: namely, first, that the goal of philosophy is the analysis of *thought*; secondly, that the study of thought is to be sharply distinguished from the study of the psychological process of *thinking*; and, finally, that the only proper method for analysing thought consists in the analysis of *language*.
> ('Can Analytical Philosophy be Systematic, and Ought it to Be?', p. 458)

Philosophy should set its sights on what is systematic and impersonal: language. From this perspective the error of past philosophy lay not in approaching its problems in terms of a false conception of mental life, but in believing them to be dependent on a conception of mental life at all.

But Wittgenstein's anti-psychologism is of a different kind. His stress on the way in which language is *used* for various purposes can be seen as a critique of the sort of separation between the semantic properties of language and the intentions of its users presupposed by the Frege–Dummett view. This tension between opposed versions of anti-psychologism remains one of analytical philosophy's most fundamental unresolved issues.

Wittgenstein is concerned to demonstrate the public dimension of mental life. Its publicity, however, is that of a shared social practice rather than the independent observability of a scientific object. Thus it is arguable that his view of mental life has more in common with continental authors such as Heidegger and Merleau-Ponty than with the neo-positivist philosophy of mind now prevalent in America (and criticized in this volume by Charles Taylor).

It must be apparent that the issues raised by the conflict between understanding and enlightenment approaches are complex – too complex to resolve in the space of an introduction. Nevertheless it seems clear, even from this brief survey, that it is now not possible, whatever conception of the philosopher's task is adopted, to defend a static, essentialist picture of rationality. Hence our ecumenical title: if there is one thing that modern philosophers from Quine to Derrida can agree upon it is The Need for Interpretation.

1

The Role of Philosophy in the Human Sciences

David Kirsh

Introduction

The sciences of man are about to enter a new stage of development. Fields such as Artificial Intelligence, cognitive psychology, cognitive sociology, ethnomethodology and sociobiology promise to transform our approach to the scientific study of man, mind and behaviour – to influence our questions, our research strategies, our methods and our long-range goals. Will philosophy have a role to play in this fundamental transformation? Should it?

The thesis I shall defend is that philosophy does have a role to play in the human sciences. Man is the most complex system we know. His biological constitution is more complicated than any other known organism, his cognitive capacities exceed anything we have yet encountered or created, and his social interactions are so complicated that no theory has been suggested that might even begin to qualify as a general theory of human social behaviour. Moreover, because belief in theories affects the way people interpret and value the world, acceptance of certain social, political and psychological theories can actually lead to changes in behaviour. Widespread acceptance of a theory about the stock market would be likely to affect stock market behaviour. Similarly, acceptance of a theory about alienation, or about neurosis, may aggravate a person's perception of these phenomena and make him more neurotic and alienated than before. Theories in the human sciences interact with their subject matter to an extent unheard of in the natural sciences. And they frequently have normative effects as well. Consequently, theorists in the human sciences focus on a system (man and his culture) that is so complex that there is no shared view of goals and methods for them to appeal to in times of dispute and conflict. At these moments scientific argument becomes so abstract as to be indistinguishable from philosophical argument, and the two subjects, philosophy and the human sciences, merge.

According to Kuhn, a science only reaches maturity by passing through an immature phase where there is overt disagreement over the fundamentals of the field. Lacking a consensus on both the legitimate problem, of the subject and the proper methods of research, scientists in immature disciplines appeal to general philosophical principles in arguing for their research strategies. Decisions concerning the relevance of certain phenomena, the propriety of importing techniques and methods developed in different fields, the desirability of providing explanations of the same type as those found in other sciences; these and more, must be justified. And in the early phase of a science there is no guarantee that all parties will make the same decision.

The human sciences are not exactly new. Anthropology, sociology, history, psychology and politics have been with us in some form or another for a long time. Still, they are sufficiently immature to foster the sorts of disputes just mentioned; and recently there have been basic disagreements concerning their *raison d'être* and their relation to other scientific research.

In what follows I shall distinguish five ways in which philosophical research can be relevant to the human sciences. No evidence will be provided to show that scientists normally do listen to philosophers, merely that attention to philosophy should be of benefit.

Methodology

Perhaps the most obvious way philosophy can contribute to the human sciences is by questioning underlying methodological principles.

Two sorts of methodological principle can be distinguished. The first sort is required if any systematic activity akin to science is to be possible at all. They are indispensable for scientific work and necessarily apply to every branch of science. Examples of such primary principles include the assumptions that nature is not chaotic, hence all phenomena are governed by laws, if only statistical; and that like causes produce like effects, which justifies the conviction that objects have stable dispositions. These principles can be regarded as the ultimate presuppositions of science, and they lead directly to general methodological directives.

Since primary principles underly all scientific research, epistemologists are deeply interested in their reliability and warrant. But it is the second species of principle that is of more immediate concern to philosophers interested in the human sciences. These secondary principles are supplementary or subsidiary to the primary set, and their denial does not entail the collapse of science.

Secondary principles serve as heuristics in the discovery process. They motivate the choice of research strategies and bias the scientist's expectations concerning the types of hypotheses that will explain the empirical regularities. Hence they may be field-specific. Examples of secondary principles are the assumptions that all regularities in nature can be represented mathematically, therefore all properties are quantifiable; that nature is in certain respects simple, hence scientists will prefer the simplest of alternative hypotheses; that nature is decomposable into a hierarchy of causal levels, where the range of laws possible at each higher level is constrained by the laws of lower levels; and that explanatory reduction between levels must always be in the direction of parts explaining whole, hence phenomena at higher levels of complexity can be ignored in explaining phenomena at lower levels of complexity. Rejection of any one of these principles would lead to a shift in research strategy and probably to a shift in the scientist's conception of what are grounds for belief in a theory. Yet rejection of a secondary principle would not mean the end of science as we know it; a scientist who rejects simplicity as a criterion for theory-selection in cognitive psychology, for instance, still carries on research in a recognizably similar manner to the physicist who accepts simplicity as an essential requirement. Thus the dispensability of secondary principles show that principles valid in one sector of science need not be valid in another. Peculiarities of subject matter may give rise to peculiarities of methodology, and one cannot assume without argument that secondary principles warranted in one field will be warranted in another.

Now one task a philosopher may undertake is to assess the reasons for expecting secondary methodological principles justified in one domain to carry across disciplinary borders. Psychologists who accepted physics as the paradigm of all good science, then, were justly challenged when asked why they thought the unique characteristics of their subject matter did not require a special methodology.

In the same vein, a number of recent criticisms offered by philosophers of human science focus on the propriety of applying methodological principles first developed in the natural sciences. Consider, for example, the methodological belief that nature is hierarchically ordered and that phenomena at lower levels may be studied without concern for phenomena at higher levels. This is certainly one of the deeper methodological prejudices among human scientists. It motivated, for instance, the sharp separation of the biological approach to human social behaviour from the psychological and sociological approaches. But is it justified? Are scientists warranted in assuming that the human world can be ordered into a hierarchy of semi-autonomous levels leading from 'human societies to organizations, to small groups, to individual human beings, to cognitive programs, in the central nervous system, to elementary information processes' (Simon, 1977, p. 247)?

There are two reasons for assuming that the apparent hierarchical structure of nature extends into the world of man. The first, a naive variant of the uniformity of nature thesis, is that, as man is part of nature, we have no reason to think that what holds throughout the rest of nature should stop at the human level. Since the assumption that nature can be decomposed into a hierarchy of semi-autonomous levels has proved of heuristic value throughout the natural sciences, the burden of proof rests on those who would deny its extension into higher levels of complexity. From physics up through chemistry, biology, neurophysiology and psychology, the best way to proceed in order to discover laws and regularities is to assume that each discipline studies its own set of entities, subject to their own set of laws. Consequently, each level can be studied in *relative* isolation from the other levels. In the natural world we can pretend that each level is more or less sealed off from other levels because the interactions taking place at each level occur at different frequencies between entities significantly different in size.

But what are the counterparts to size and frequency at the human level? A person may have interactions with an immense bureaucratic organization in roughly the way he might with another person. Moreover, his interactions are largely unaffected by the spatial distance between them. In the natural world, however, relatively intense interaction implies relative spatial closeness. The forces that seem to operate at any level work at spatial distances that are commensurate with the size of the object. Thus sub-nuclear forces can effectively be ignored at the level of molecular interaction. But, in the social world, intensive communications can take place over great distances, and degree of interaction will frequently not vary with distance. The correlation between size and frequency breaks down at the social level. Thus, although the uniformity of nature was to warrant expecting a hierarchical structure in the social world, the difference between the physical and the social world is a good reason to reject the uniformity thesis.

The second reason for assuming the human world to be ordered hierarchically is a stronger one; namely, that natural selection favours hierarchical structures. If we suppose that natural selection is the means by which complex systems evolve, then, since natural selection favours hierarchical structures, the human world will be hierarchically organized.

In 'The Architecture of Complexity', Herbert Simon explained why there is a greater probability that chance interactions will construct a system made out of stable sub-assemblies than one made out of more elementary units. The proof can be given mathematically, but the basic idea can be shown in a parable.

Simon's parable was of two watchmakers, Hora and Tempus, who assembled watches of a thousand parts each. Hora designed his watch so that he puts together sub-assemblies of about ten units each. Ten of these sub-assemblies, again, can be put together into a larger sub-assembly, and a system of ten of the latter constitutes the whole watch. Tempus, on the other hand, has developed no such design. If we assume that both watchmakers are periodically interrupted by callers, and that once interrupted they lose their place in the assembly they were just working on, it is clear that Hora will finish a watch long before Tempus, for each disruption will cost Hora at most the time to redo the sub-sub-assembly of ten pieces that he was currently working on; while Tempus will have to start from scratch. Tempus will never succeed in assembling a watch – he will suffer the fate of Sisyphus: as often as he rolls the rock up the hill, it will roll down again (cf. Simon, 1969, 1977).

Assuming Simon's proof to be valid, we can expect that nature will be filled with systems that are decomposable into sub-systems. Indeed, biological evolution would be impossible unless natural selection could improve some sub-systems without affecting others. In one sense, all biological creatures can be seen as organized conglomerations of modules. Each module links up with certain others, and providing that it serves its function in the overall system, it can, for certain purposes, be treated as a relatively independent unit. Efficiency in evolution, therefore, demands that the human world be decomposable into sub-systems where the interactions between individuals or entities inside the system are stronger and more frequent than ones with individuals or entities outside the system. But does it follow that the ordering at the human level will be hierarchical? The fact that individuals can interact with corporations, or bureaucracies, etc., seems to militate against that idea. Much more importantly, a corollary of the principle of hierarchic structure is that parts can be studied in relative isolation from the whole, and that where reductive explanations are possible they should explain the whole in terms of its parts. But can individual persons be studied separately from the society they belong to? Can social regularities be viewed as the outcome of individual actions?

A familiar strategy in fields like economics and sociology is to assume that individual persons are ideally rational agents. If one wants to study group interaction, it has been found useful to assume that the participants are all rational beings with goals and beliefs, who strive in the most rational way to achieve those goals, given the constraints of their situation. Research is carried on as if rational beings form an autonomous level of the hierarchy.

By taking man to be a rational being, human scientists believe they can find meaningful generalizations about human behaviour without attending to details at cognitive or sub-rational levels, and without concern for regularities that hold at higher levels, in the group of society as a whole. The idea is that if a person is well adapted to his environment then he will tend to respond to that environment rationally. It doesn't matter how he actually succeeds in doing this: one simply assumes that he has whatever cognitive machinery is necessary for success. Only if something goes wrong at the cognitive level would a study of the sophisticated processes underpinning rational conduct be relevant. Normally one may ignore them. Similarly, it doesn't matter how his actions contribute to group regularities, for it is assumed that his individual actions may be studied in abstraction from the society to which he belongs. All that is required is a specification of the environment in which he finds himself.

The type of rational man approach being described is one which fits with the methodological assumption of universal hierarchy. But can it be made to work? Is there really no interaction between the rational level and higher levels? Since an agent's actions are rational only relative to some environment E, it must be possible to provide (1) a precise definition of each E that the agent may be in; and (2) a method for deciding of any possible action A in E whether or not A is a rational act. Unless these two requirements are met there will be cases where there is no well defined rational action for the agent to perform. Requirement (1) assumes that the agent's world can be objectively partitioned into a system of task or problem environments. Requirement (2) assumes that there is an objective method of deciding the rational action in every possible environment that the agent might be in. Together they set down the conditions for approaching man as a rational being.

Both these assumptions are highly questionable. Most of the more important tasks or problems we confront are not undertaken in well structured environments. There is continual scope for innovating means to achieve our ends, and the rules constraining our alternatives are much freer than (1) demands. But let us assume for argument's sake that (1) can be achieved: that is, let us assume that the agent can be treated as a being who moves from one type of chess game to another. Is it plausible to suppose that there could be a culturally invariant conception of rationality as demanded by (2)? Is there always an objectively best course of action which all societies would recognize?

Cultural invariance in rationality is required by the hierarchy model because if we were to allow rational agents in different societies to hold different conceptions of how to act rationally we would lose whatever chance we had of studying their conduct without considering their psychological processes or their society's conventions. We would cease treating the rational level as an autonomous level. Of course alien cultures may have different norms of thought. But insofar as these are conventional, their maintenance is explained in terms of the rational expectations agents hold about each other's conduct. Hence since rationality explains cultural norms it must be independent of culture. Yet should this not be an empirical discovery? Are the *a priori* arguments for defending the cultural invariance of rationality sound?

The problems surrounding these issues rapidly become philosophical. But then philosophy is relevant to methodology.

Defining the phenomena

The second major way in which philosophy can serve the human sciences is by helping to define the phenomena. When a science is not yet mature, and theorists have still to build up a stock of technical, theoretical and observational terms, questions must be raised in ordinary, pre-theoretical language. Philosophy can serve to explicate the expressions being used.

Terms like cognition, rationality, representation, social, judgement, perception and thinking, for example, are umbrella terms that designate a more or less well defined class of phenomena. Before a theory of rationality or judgement can be developed, the phenomena to be explained must be at least roughly identified. And so appeal is made to a pre-theoretical classification. As theories emerge, however, more precise ways of describing the observational domain will be suggested and reasons will be given for grouping a class of phenomena together into a unified subject. As Kuhn emphasized, once a field has a dominant theory, scientists can pursue selected phenomena in more detail, designing special equipment for research and working more systematically than before.

Yet if we wish to question the adequacy of a given theory we need to be able to refer to the phenomena independently of the theory which specifies them. If theory T defines the range of the phenomena which it will explain, then, although we can still discover well defined phenomena that falsify T, there would be no way of showing that T fails to explain all the *relevant* phenomena. The domain of relevant phenomena would be co-extensive with the range of phenomena explicable by T. And that means that there would be no scope for criticizing the theory on the grounds of completeness.

In advanced sciences, theorists have their own internal ways of deciding whether a theory is complete or not. But in the human sciences debates about the relevance of certain phenomena still rely on distinctions introduced by common sense.

Rational decision theory provides a good example of a scientific theory which can be criticized on common-sense grounds. The theory of rational choice provides a calculus for deciding the rationality of any action. Given a specification of the options a person sees open to him, and the valuations he places on each, the theory specifies what his most rational act would be. It does not describe what he will do, merely what he would do, were he to act rationally. But there is a strong presumption that, as people often do act rationally, application of rational decision theory can predict their behaviour.

The primary weakness of rational decision theory is that not all activities which people rationally pursue readily fit into its quantitative schema. Common sense has supplied us with a rich set of distinctions to understand the diverse ways in which people can act rationally. In particular, actions which we rationalize by appeal to moral rules, actions which we accept as part of our social role, and actions which we perform because they strike us as dignified or respectable, appear especially hard to represent as the result of applying a sharply defined principle of rationality to a set of weighted alternatives. It is easier to explain these actions *qualitatively* as the result of some process of practical reasoning, as being actions which are seen as *reasonable* or *appropriate* in the light of an understanding of the situation. Moreover, questions about the rationality of actions also arise in problem solving situations. My next move in a chess game may be more or less rational. But again it is hard to judge the rationality of acts in problem situations by using rational decision theory methods. The theory is too narrow to handle these sorts of rational acts. These considerations do not refute the theory, but they do suggest that the theory is incomplete and must either be extended or supplemented by other models of rational decision-making.

Conceptual analysis

A third way philosophy can serve the human sciences is by subjecting common sense concepts to philosophical analysis in order to decide whether they could become good scientific concepts. For example, one well entrenched debate concerns whether our ordinary concepts of belief, desire, meaning and thought are the right kind of concepts to enter into scientific explanations. Are they applied in ways which suggest they designate entities in the causal order? If not, then what is the status of explanations in which they appear?

Alfred Schutz, the noted phenomenological sociologist, has argued that 'all scientific explanations of the social world *can*, and for certain purposes *must*, refer to the subjective meanings of the action of human beings' (Dallmayr and McCarthy, pp. 235–6). It is the job of the social scientist, he suggests, to compile a comprehensive view of the objects of belief, thought and desire that agents have when acting. These objects are not merely sentences to which individual agents would assent: they are conceptualized states of affairs, propositions; they are the contents of thought and can in principle be shared by people across languages. As he puts it.

> the observational field of the social scientist – social reality – has a specific meaning and relevance structure for the human beings living, acting and thinking within it. By a series of common-sense constructs they have pre-selected and pre-interpreted this world which they experience as the reality of their daily lives. *It is these thought objects of theirs which determine their behaviour* by motivating it. The thought objects constructed by the social scientist, in order to grasp this social reality, have to be founded upon the thought objects constructed by the common-sense thinking of men, living their daily life within their social world.
> (Schutz, p. 223, my emphasis)

The central claim Schutz makes is that all human action makes sense within the context of each agent's mental representation of the social world. To understand this internal representation it is necessary to explore the concepts the agent uses to describe and structure his environment. Hence the scientist must not substitute for the agent's common-sense concepts technical ones he has generated himself. Once research has revealed the agent's subjective view of the world it ought to be possible to understand or rationalize his actions – provided, of course, that the scientist can recognize what counts as rational within the agent's framework. If this proviso is met then attributions of propositional attitudes to agents are also true. Consequently, beliefs, desires and thoughts must exist, and failing a reason to think otherwise, they must be items in the causal order.

Recent work in the cognitive sciences also assumes that agents have mental representations, and that true statements can be made about them. Chomsky, for instance, holds that by 'assuming the existence of abstract mental representations and interpretive operations of [a grammatical and phonological] sort, we can find a surprising degree of organization underlying what appears superficially to be a chaotic arrangement of data, and in certain cases we can also explain why linguistic expressions are heard, used, and understood in certain ways' (*Language and Mind*, p. 43). Chomskian competence implies mastery of rules, and hence presupposes a system which deals with discrete symbols, and which can apply rules and transformations on those symbols. The symbols are not merely fictional constructs, they are meant to be real entities, and true statements can be made about them.

Yet despite these claims by phenomenological sociologists and cognitive scientists to be studying the beliefs, thoughts and mental representations of agents, the philosopher may ask whether they are the *same* beliefs, thoughts and mental representations we refer to when normally using these terms. Scientists often dismiss this question with an aside, suggesting that if all that is at issue is the names of terms then they will rename these states. But this reply misses the point. Our everyday concepts have evolved in our culture to serve certain purposes. In particular, ascriptions of responsibility in legal and moral discussions depend on the beliefs, desires and intentions attributed to agents, and, as the human sciences advance, it is assumed that they will help in making such judgements more sound. Already, psychologists are being brought into law courts to discuss issues of criminal responsibility and to decide whether the accused is fit to plead. Moreover, the standards by which laws are written and enforced, actions rewarded and punished, and goals set and accepted as reasonable, derive from a loose consensus about what agents normally desire, and what they can be expected to know. Were there to be a significant change in our attribution of attitudes, our entire politico-legal system would change. But all these applications of theory would be impossible if the beliefs and desires which scientists talk about have nothing to do with beliefs and desires as ordinarily construed. The assumption that the cognitive and human sciences could inform our social decisions depends on assuming that the taxonomies of mental states we have developed for our social needs can be correlated with the mental states described in the cognitive and human sciences. Yet what is the grounding for that belief?

Correlations between taxonomic systems can only be established if the predicates in each system are well defined. Clearly, what is required is an analysis of our ordinary concepts. Perhaps, as Quine

has suggested, we will decide that our ordinary concepts of propositional attitudes suffer from a vagueness and ambiguity that make
them unfit for interesting correlations with scientific predicates. If we
do not know the degree of variation we are allowed in describing the
contents of a belief, then in what sense does that belief have a definite
content? These are questions the philosopher must ask. Pending an
answer, there is no principled reason to think that psychological
theories can serve our social interests.

Pragmatic considerations

I have just stated that prior to an analysis of our ordinary terms we
cannot know whether psychological or sociological theories will be
relevant to our moral and legal concerns. Can philosophers provide
arguments that show that theories in the human sciences ought to be?

The standard view of science is that the point of theorizing is to
discover the true, or approximately true structure of reality. This
purely theoretical goal can be pursued, it is held, independently of any
practical applications which a theory may have. There is no reason to
demand that applications constrain theory: if a particular theory does
not deliver the laws and explanations required for a given practical
end, the engineer, politician, psychiatrist or whoever wants to use the
theory will just have to look elsewhere for guidance. The theory itself
is no worse for that. For practical applications are no theoretical
virtue. Hence, on this view, psychologists and social theorists must be
free to devise whatever models they hold to be closest to the truth. It is
pointless to demand that they construct theories that answer questions first raised in other disciplines

Accordingly, cognitive or social theories cannot be criticized on the
grounds that they operate with theoretical concepts which cannot be
translated into terms that are meaningful to politicians or judges. To
maintain that they ought to use other concepts implies that they
should serve interests other than truth. And this is anti-scientific. As
Fodor says,

> the states of the organism postulated in theories of cognition
> would not count as states of the organism for purposes of, say, a
> theory of legal or moral responsibility. But so what? What mat-
> ters is that they should count as states of the organism for *some*

useful purpose. In particular, what matters is that they should count as states of the organism *for purposes of constructing psychological theories that are true.*
(*The Language of Thought*, p. 53, my emphasis)

Truth, then, is considered by many theorists to be the overarching goal of scientific research. A concern for practical applications is secondary and should not significantly constrain research strategy. For this reason, allegations that truth is not attainable in the human sciences, or that it should play a secondary role in theory selection, threaten to upset standard methodological preconceptions. What sort of objectivity can one hope to obtain, if truth is impossible? How can non-true theories be rationally preferred?

There are two philosophical arguments to show that truth could not be the proper objective of theories in the human sciences. The first derives from Quine's thesis of the 'indeterminacy of translation'. The second derives from the conviction that research into the nature of social reality changes social reality. Both support essentially the same conclusion: in the human sciences, theories must serve social interests. Truth, and objectivity, as normally construed, are the wrong properties to demand. Let us consider each argument in turn.

Quine's original thesis was a claim about theories of language. But it applies equally to any social or psychological theory which uses interpretations of verbal behaviour as data. His basic idea was that theories of language-structure and language-meaning do not describe determinate features of the world. Linguistic theories purport to describe an objective linguistic reality, but there are no genuine facts concerning meaning or syntactic structure to constitute such a reality. Agreement in linguistic judgement therefore can only give the *illusion* that there is an objective subject matter being judged; in fact there is no determinate structure underpinning those judgements. A correct understanding of linguistic phenomena, then, would recognize that sentences can be understood in different ways for different purposes, no one way being absolutely true or right.

If Quine is right, it follows that any theory that is tested by interpreting verbal behaviour cannot strictly be true. Thus, since many theories in the human sciences are tested by assessing the replies which subjects make to questionnaires, they cannot be true.

This conclusion was arrived at in the following manner. Assume that a social scientist operates with an implicit theory of interpretation in much the way that other scientists operate with implicit theories of measurement. Then social theories are related to interpreted data (I-data) as non-social theories are related to measured or observational data (O-data). Following this line, a social theory may be more or less confirmed by the available I-data just as a non-social theory may be more or less confirmed by the available O-data. Similarly, a social theory may be underdetermined by all possible I-data, just as a non-social theory may be underdetermined by all possible O-data. But, whereas we assume that O-data are either true or false, the thesis of indeterminacy of translation states that I-data, especially of the sort obtained by interpreting the replies to questionnaires, could not possibly be true or false. According to Quine, there are simply too many different but equally satisfactory ways of interpreting those replies to warrant thinking that any one of them is the right or absolutely true way. There is no such thing as truth in interpretation. But then the evidence or I-data which support social theories cannot be literally true.

Yet if the evidence for a theory is not true, how can the theory itself be true? According to a standard conception of confirmation, when data confirm a theory, the theory entails those data. But, since the data that confirm a social theory cannot be true, the theory itself cannot be true, for all the consequences of a true theory must themselves be true. Accordingly, although we can still judge the empirical adequacy of a social theory, relative to a set of I-data, we cannot say that an empirically adequate theory could ever be a true theory.

This is not, of course, to say that the theory is falsified. A theory is falsified when it is inconsistent with (true) data. But in the case we are envisaging, the theory entails the data and so cannot be inconsistent with it (as long as the theory is not self-contradictory). Nonetheless, the theory still is not true, for the data themselves are not true. Hence, if the thesis of the indeterminacy of translation is correct, theories based on interpretations of verbal behaviour can never be true. The indeterminacy which infects linguistic theory extends throughout all the sciences which rely on interpretations of sentences – which is to say almost all theories in the human sciences.

To bring out the motivation for this extraordinary view, let us contrast it with the sort of position it is arguing against. According to a realist, like Fodor, the primary function of language is to communicate ideas. A speaker is assumed to have an idea or message in mind which he intends to communicate. This thought is held to be internally represented by the speaker in the form of a sentence in an inner language, which is then translated by the speaker into a linguistic utterance which he believes the hearer will understand. When communication is successful, the hearer translates the utterance back into a thought of the same type as the speaker intended to communicate. Communication, therefore, is seen to consist in establishing a correspondence between the mental states of the speaker and those of the hearer. The goal of the linguist is to state for any communication just what the content and structure of the exchanged thought is.

On Fodor's account then, linguistic theories not only purport to describe an objective linguistic reality, they may actually succeed. In sharp contrast to Quine, Fodor believes that there is a true way to interpret a sentence: the way which best reflects the structure and meaning of the thought which the speaker had intended to communicate. Social theories supported by I-data, then, can be literally true, just as theories in the natural sciences can be true. For once it is granted that theories of interpretation can be true, the I-data they generate become good scientific data, on equal footing with O-data. Consequently, disputes between social scientists over the proper interpretation of certain sentences are no different in principle from disputes between natural scientists over the proper description of highly theory-laden observations. In both cases, disputes arise because the scientists have different theoretical commitments. But, according to Fodor, in both cases there is a fact of the matter.

Now in Quine's opinion this account cannot be correct. Firstly, if there is any indeterminacy in translation between different languages at the public level, it reappears at the private level between the sentences in the inner language and the public sentences into which they are translated. How, then, can thoughts, which therefore are doubly indeterminate from a hearer's perspective, be used to lessen the indeterminacy of public translation? Secondly, he maintains that this entire way of viewing communication is based on such a deep misunderstanding of the relation of thought to language that it utterly mis-states what the linguist can do.

From Quine's perspective the linguist can never provide a theory which states for each utterance the precise meaning and structure of the thought which allegedly gave rise to it, because the best description of the meaning and structure of a thought is given by the best description of the meaning and structure of the sentence that expresses it – and there is always more than one way of describing that. If Quine is correct in assuming that there is no method for discovering the structure and meaning of a thought except through analysing the sentence which expresses it, then one certainly cannot assume an antecedent knowledge of the thought in order to choose between different interpretations of the public sentences. The order of accessibility is from language to thought, not vice versa. Thus, if a sentence can be interpreted in many ways, each way equally justified by the linguistic data, then the thought must be interpretable in many ways too. Any ineliminable ambiguity in structure and meaning that a sentence has, necessarily applies to the thought. Hence thought and talk cannot be separated as Fodor seems to suggest. The study of thought *just is* the study of talk.

Unfortunately, the matter is not so simple. Fodor can accept part of this criticism and still affirm his main thesis. Admission of a logical connection between a thought and the sentence that correctly expresses it is acceptable to a mentalist, like Fodor, so long as it is understood that on *any particular occasion* it is a contingent matter whether the speaker accurately expresses his thoughts. It is unquestionable that thoughts are logically connected to the sentences which correctly express them. How else could we specify our thoughts? The questionable issue is whether it makes sense to say that a speaker has a determinate thought in mind which he can mis-express.

Fodor argues that it does make sense. If all the data of verbal and non-verbal behaviour and all the information we can extract about the subject by applying psychological techniques are brought to bear on the question of mental contents, it is his opinion that we ought to be able to single out a determinate causal state of the speaker as the thought behind his words. It would then be possible to specify its precise structure and meaning.

Quine, on the other hand, is obliged to argue that it makes no sense to talk of determinate inner thoughts at all. The entire model of thoughts inside the head is misguided. Although it is true enough to say that a thought may be ill-stated, what is meant is not that a thought inside one's head fails to correspond to what is said. It is to say that there are formulations available which better capture one's intentions. One should not infer from this, however, that there are thoughts which are well formed and determinate residing in one's head, awaiting proper expression. Thoughts no more explain why a speaker utters a certain sentence than phlogiston explains why a certain object burns. Neither explains because neither exists.

Consequently, Quine's attitude towards linguistic theory, and therefore all theories relying on a theory of interpretation, must be instrumentalist. Thoughts, meanings and syntactic structures may look like genuine theoretical entities for they appear in what at first look like explanatory theories of linguistic behaviour. But in fact, analysis of evidence and methodology shows that they cannot be causal entities at all. There is no way of rendering those notions sufficiently empirical to make them designate determinate entities in the casual order. Theories which rely on them can be used to codify and predict data, but we must not pretend that they provide us with insight into a world of thoughts, meanings and linguistic structures. No such world exists.

Thus, if one were to accept with Quine that indeterminacy plagues every theory which relies on linguistic phenomena as evidence, most theories in the social and cognitive sciences would have no determinate truth value. Choice of a theory would be justifiable only on the grounds that it leads to effective prediction, control or to attaining other practical goals. Truth as a theoretical virtue would be displaced.

What, then, should be made of Fodor's claim that psychological theories need not be answerable to any interests beside truth? The answer has been well stated by the psychologist John Anderson.

> The fact that it is not possible to uniquely determine cognitive structures and processes poses a clear limitation on our ability to understand the nature of human intelligence. The realization of this fact has also led to a shift in my personal goals. I am less interested in defending the exact assumptions of a theory and am more interested in evolving some theory that can account for important empirical phenomena. By a theory that accounts for 'important empirical phenomena' I mean one that addresses real world issues as well as laboratory phenomena. Such real world issues for [Anderson's computer theory] would include how to improve people's ability to learn and use language, to learn and remember text, to reason, and to solve problems. *This reflects my belief that the final arbiter of a cognitive theory is going to be its utility in practical application.*
> (*Language, Meaning and Thought*, pp. 16–17, my emphasis)

For Anderson, application has surpassed the truth as the cardinal goal of theories in cognitive psychology.

The second argument to establish the importance of pragmatic considerations in the human sciences arises out of the interaction which takes place between theories of mind or society and the minds or societies they are about.

If a social theory cannot be tested without affecting the society it is about, then no social theory can ever be confirmed as an accurate characterization of the society as it would have been had it not been observed. Furthermore, because the availability of social theories may radically alter social conditions, additional complications enter into the assessment of social theories. For instance, the widespread knowledge of theories of stockmarket behaviour may help cause the changes described. How, then, can truth be the goal of social theories where self-fulfilling prophecies are a real possibility?

Many physicists believe that where observation necessarily affects the system under study, attempts to characterize it as it is in its unobserved state, unaffected by any probe, are misconceived. The system as it is in itself is too ill-defined to be a scientific notion; one is required to work within the constraints imposed by the need for verification. At first, the problem of interaction at the social level may seem to be analogous. But there is a difference between the observer-object interactions occurring at the physical level and the observer-object interactions at the social level. For, at the social level, the observer may actually affect the mechanism by which the agent decides what he will do in the future.

Imagine, for instance, an anthropologist setting out to codify the rules of some ritual. We may suppose that it is a complex ritual and he has to ask the natives about it. He begins by setting down all the rules which the natives know they observe. He then studies their practice minutely to see if there are other rules which they might be observing unwittingly. As his characterization becomes more detailed, he may wonder whether some regularity, a gesture perhaps, is a genuine rule-governed part of the ritual or merely an accidental recurrence. Is it a coincidence that the natives perform that gesture in those circumstances? Is it relevant to the ritual? If the anthropologist then asks the natives about the gesture, they may decide to incorporate it as a formal element in their practice and sincerely contend that it was part of the ritual all along. Similarly, if he asks the natives how they apply their rules in hard cases, they may make a snap decision, sharpen the rule and keep to it in the future. How can he decide whether or not they have changed the rules of the ritual? Is there a fact of the matter?

In the example cited, each participant in the ritual now has a more explicit understanding of his practice. His pre-reflective understanding has been exchanged for an explicit self-awareness and this added awareness affects the way he will make decisions. In social theories, then, interaction can actually bias the probabilities that a theory is predictively adequate. In cases where the interpretations a theorist offers affect the way his subjects understand their social world, his theory can become a self-fulfilling prophecy, guaranteeing the truth of its predictions. But then different theories could have been predictively adequate if different anthropologists had got to the tribe first.

What is the place of truth in such theories? There is no easy answer. Some philosophers believe that truth becomes wholly secondary. Since the anthropologist cannot think he is really studying the ritual as it is in its natural setting, he must, presumably, allow that his theory is of the ritual as it is after his tampering. But since his tampering may have considerable effects on the social order, his theories are not simply descriptive theories, they have normative consequences. A different anthropologist who asked different questions might have encouraged the natives to see their society in a different light, with the consequences that desirable social change occurred. One suggestion, therefore, is that social theories be judged partly by their normative effects. Another suggestion is that normative elements be ignored and efforts be made to understand in greater detail the mechanism by which the anthropologist changed the society studied. If enough is known about the natives' psychology then *perhaps* the impact which the anthropologist makes can be subtracted from the natives' practices. In this situation we can extrapolate backwards and give a true description of what their practices were in their natural state. This, at any rate, is one belief a theorist might hold.

To sum up, any philosophical argument which succeeds in demonstrating that truth is not the right objective in the human sciences ought to have significant scientific repercussions. If a philosopher can show the scientist that the goals of his enterprise are not what he once thought, he has raised an issue that must have methodological consequences. The claim we considered is that a *good* interpretation of social behaviour is not the same as a *true* interpretation. I have not defended either of the arguments to show that this claim is true. I have, however, tried to show how acceptance of these philosophical arguments could lead to a change in scientific practice, and an acceptance of the need for more pragmatic considerations in research policy.

Awkward questions

The final way in which philosophers can contribute to the development of the human sciences is by raising questions and problems from a philosophical standpoint which may provoke theorists in the field to re-examine their basic conceptual presuppositions. Some of the subjects philosophers study are also studied by human scientists. These shared subjects include the nature of reasoning, understanding, social interaction, rationality, judgement and perception. The credibility of philosophical accounts of these subjects derives not only from the light they cast on the empirical phenomena but also from the way they fit together with other philosophical accounts. It is a constraint on a philosophical account that it be consistent with other philosophical accounts thought credible. Thus a certain philosophical account of judgement is to be preferred if it links up with the most credible epistemological theory of perception, and, better yet, if it connects well with the most plausible metaphysical thesis about the nature of the human subject.

Now if a psychological or anthropological inquiry were to turn up conclusions which discredited one or another of these philosophical doctrines, it is likely that it would have ramifications in other philosophical fields as well. But since a scientific theory is tested by its consequences, and since some of the consequences of scientific theories in the human sciences are philosophical, it may be possible to 'test' a given theory in the human sciences by assessing its philosophical consequences. If a theory generates a philosophical paradox, or challenges deeply held metaphysical convictions, the most reasonable thing to do may be to fault the scientific framework which generates it. Such a framework may solve a number of immediate problems, but may contain a basic inadequacy which will frustrate the long-run development of the field.

The premise underlying this suggestion is that the presence of a philosophical problem is evidence that there is some difficulty in the received way of thinking about the subject matter. The problem arises because the proposed theoretical framework is an inadequate way of representing the subject. Hence it is possible to generate inconsistencies, paradoxes, unanswerable questions or bizarre conclusions.

A clear case where a recent scientific theory generated an undesirable philosophical consequence – more precisely, where a scientific theory appeared to support a philosophical thesis that had been discredited – can be found in some of the scientific theories of perception devised in the fifties and early sixties.

During the heyday of communication theory in psychology, it was popular to interpret perceiving as a kind of internal observation of incoming signals from the sense organs. Conscious experience was thought to consist in the mind's witnessing certain neural events, in much the way that a radar technician witnesses the changes on a display screen. The senses were interpreted as information channels containing filters, and processors, which brought all data to a neural 'terminal' where it was displayed as a coherent whole for the mind to scan. The information would then pass on to a decision-making component where a decision would be made concerning how to move the body given the goals and objectives of the organism. If thoughts were involved in these latter processes the mind might scan their progression. In either case, though, the mind was thought to do no more than inspect finished processes; it did not seem involved in the processing of sensory data or in putting thought-fragments together into thoughts. Its role was passive.

In fact, most psychological models did not make explicit reference to a mind. The mind was not a well defined entity and so its postulation could serve no genuinely explanatory function. Nonetheless, the concept of a mind scanning the brain haunted most of the theories of the time. (Cf. D.M. Mackay, 'The Mind's Eye View of the Brain', 1965, pp. 479-483.)

By the late fifties, however, philosophers had utterly rejected the idea of the mind as an inner witness of the brain. It led to inconsistencies, paradoxes, and bizarre conclusions. Bringing these problems to the attention of scientists was not sufficient to convince them that the general framework for theories of perception was faulty. But the arguments did indicate that intrinsic limitations to the approach were likely to be found; and on this occasion history proved the philosopher right.

In general, whenever changes in philosophical theory are not in step with changes in science, there is scope for philosopher and scientist to enter into a dialogue. The result of such interdisciplinary discussions may be that both philosophical and scientific thinking are improved.

Conclusion

The idea that philosophical considerations could actually carry weight in scientific research may seem to misrepresent the nature of philosophy. Philosophical truth, it has been said, must be discovered *a priori*, its conclusions must be analytic. The proper task of philosophy, therefore, must be confined to explicating meaning, checking the validity of inferences and offering logical translations and paraphrases of statements. None of these activities directly affects science. Others have maintained that philosophers can help to clarify scientific problems in their early phase, but once problems are well structured they become susceptible to empirical methodology and the philosopher drops out. Thus questions first raised by philosophers are co-opted by experimentalists. Either way, the role of philosophy in science is minimized. Philosophy remains external to the field.

I have tried to show that these conceptions of philosophy do not do justice to the variety of philosophical arguments. As Collingwood argued half a century ago, every science rests on a set of 'ultimate presuppositions' which provide the framework within which it is conducted at any period. Exposing some of these underlying beliefs helps to place research in a wider context. I suggested that this is one task a philosopher is qualified to undertake. A scientist is not likely to follow a particular line of thought if he has conceptual reasons for thinking he is pursuing a chimera. Similarly, if he has reason to suspect that his methodology is biased, or otherwise logically faulty, he will want to reconsider the worth of his theories. A philosopher who brings outside considerations to the attention of scientists creates a dialogue about the foundation of their field. In clarifying the nature of this dialogue, I claimed that philosophers could help scientists to assess their methodological assumptions, remind them of their goals and their obligation to relate theoretical discoveries to common-sense beliefs, and ask scientists awkward questions exposing unacknowledged philosophical commitments. The outcome, we hope, would be better science.[1]

2

Creation and Discovery: Wittgenstein on Conceptual Change

Christopher M. Leich

I

Throughout his later work on the philosophy of mathematics, Wittgenstein advances the surprising idea that the progress of mathematics involves continual conceptual change. Most often, he puts the idea in terms of mathematical *proof*: a new proof, he tells us, 'creates' a new concept (*RFM* III/41) or 'determines' a new concept (*RFM* III/31); it 'changes grammar', and introduces a 'new criterion' (*RFM* III/24).[1] But it is very plausible to suppose that these claims about mathematical proof are the products of a more general view of *mathematically necessary truth*: the view that one can grasp a mathematically necessary truth (e.g. that $5+7=12$) for the first time only at the expense of a change in one's concepts (of, e.g., 5, or 7, or addition). Wittgenstein links mathematical necessity with conceptual change explicitly:

> The mathematical Must is only another expression of the fact that mathematics forms concepts. (*RFM* V/46)
> This *must* shows that he has adopted a concept. (*RFM* VI/18)
> What is the transition I make from 'it will be like this' to 'it *must* be like this'? I form a different concept. (*RFM* III/29)

And these points are associated with the idea that if one is undecided about a certain mathematical claim, one does not *understand* the claim. Thus, in Wittgenstein's view no one now understands Fermat's (undecided) Last Theorem:

> If I am to know what a proposition like Fermat's last theorem says, must I not know what the criterion is, for the proposition to

be true? I am not [acquainted] with any criterion for the truth of this proposition (*RFM* VI/13)

Hence, coming to grasp a new mathematical truth involves a change in one's understanding:

> The question arises: Can't we be mistaken in thinking that we understand a question?
>
> For many mathematical proofs do lead us to say that we cannot imagine something which we believed that we could imagine. (E.g., the construction of the heptagon.) (*PI* I/517)

The picture that emerges, then, seems to be as follows. In Wittgenstein's view, if one does not know whether a certain mathematical claim is true, one's concepts must be somehow deficient, so deficient that one cannot be described as understanding the claim fully. More generally, if one does not know whether or not a certain claim is true as a matter of mathematical necessity, one's grasp of what it means is deficient. Solving a mathematical problem, i.e. coming to grasp that a certain claim is true as a matter of mathematical necessity, thus always involves a conceptual change, or a change in one's understanding. Unsolved mathematical problems – e.g. Goldbach's celebrated Conjecture that every even number is the sum of two primes – are conceptually unclear. Because we do not know whether the Conjecture is true, we do not know now what it *means* to say 'Every even number is the sum of two primes'.

This remarkable view of Wittgenstein's will be the focus of this essay. For the most part, I shall be exploring the view's motivation. I shall argue that motivation is not lacking, appearances to the contrary notwithstanding: rather, the view is the product of a set of deep reflections on understanding and necessity, reflections which cannot be dismissed out of hand. But before I attempt to explain what these reflections are, I should like first to develop the view itself a little more clearly. If we are to appreciate its force, we must be clear about what it does and does not involve.

II

Because Wittgenstein's claims about conceptual change make use of the concept of mathematical necessity, one must be careful, when reflecting on his view, to distinguish between sentences (e.g. '5+7=12') and what sentences express (e.g. (that) 5+7=12). It is true that Wittgenstein himself did not spend much time on this distinction in his later work; indeed, he even used the same word ('*Satz*' in his German writings, 'proposition' in his English ones) to refer sometimes to a sentence, and sometimes to what a sentence expresses. But it would be wrong to interpret this liberal usage as a licence to ignore the distinction.

In order to see why, let us focus first on the following claim, which I shall call (W):

> If one does not know whether or not a certain sentence expresses a mathematically necessary truth, one does not understand the sentence.

(W) affords us one way of capturing Wittgenstein's claims about conceptual change. It implies that we do not now understand the sentence 'Every even number is the sum of two primes', for we do not know whether or not that sentence expresses a mathematically necessary truth. Hence also (W) implies that we can come to grasp that the sentence does express such a truth, or that it does not, only by dint of a change in our understanding.

There are, I believe, stronger claims than (W) to which Wittgenstein would have subscribed in expounding his view. But we do not need to investigate these claims here; for present purposes, it is enough that Wittgenstein would have subscribed to (W). What needs to be stressed now is instead a negative point: whatever else one may say in attempting to sum up Wittgenstein's claims about conceptual change, one must not depart from (W) in one's treatment of the bearers of necessary truth. In (W), what sentences express, rather than sentences themselves, are seen as the bearers of necessary truth. Thus, only what '5+7=12' expresses (viz. (that) 5+7=12) is treated as a mathematically necessary truth; '5+7=12' itself is not. It would be quite wrong to suppose that this distinction is not an important one, and so to suppose that Wittgenstein's view might equally well be summed up by the following claim, which I shall call (A):

> If one does not know whether or not a certain sentence is a

mathematically necessary truth, one does not understand the sentence.

The trouble with (A) is not that it is false, or even that Wittgenstein would not have accepted it. The trouble is rather than even if it were true and acceptable to Wittgenstein, it would not capture the thought that we do not now understand, e.g., Goldbach's Conjecture. (A) would capture that idea only if we had to concede that we do not know whether or not 'Every even number is the sum of two primes' is true as a matter of mathematical necessity. But there is no reason whatsoever to suppose that we now have to concede any such thing. On the contrary, it looks as though we can be confident that whatever mathematical progress is made, the sentence 'Every even number is the sum of two primes' will remain if true only contingently true. For we can be confident quite generally, in advance of any progress in mathematics, that *any* given mathematical sentence (or indeed any sentence at all) can be at best only contingently true.

A few simple facts underwrite this confidence. First, if one decides to treat truth as a property of sentences at all, rather than a property of what sentences express, then one must agree that the truth of a sentence can vary with what it expresses. Thus, if the sentence '$5+7=12$' is true, one must agree that it would have been false, had it meant e.g. that $5+7=13$. But, secondly, it is surely mathematically contingent that a given sentence means what it does: '$5+7=12$' *might* have meant that $5+7=13$. What a given sentence means is a mathematically contingent matter, if anything is. Yet if this is correct, then it can only be mathematically contingent that a given sentence is true. If '$5+7=12$' had meant that $5+7=13$, it would have been false; but '$5+7=12$' might have meant that $5+7=13$, and therefore it *could* have been false.[2]

There is no reason to suppose that Wittgenstein himself was in any doubt on this point. It is true that he sometimes uses '*Satz*' to refer to sentences, and that he sometimes (though rarely) speaks of 'necessary *Sätze*'. But, as I noted above, '*Satz*' is multivalent; Wittgenstein does also employ it to refer to what sentences express. Read in the latter way, talk of 'necessary *Sätze*' poses no problem; the points just made do not count against the idea that what a sentence expresses can be necessarily true.

There are, then, solid grounds for thinking that (A) cannot serve to summarize Wittgenstein's views about conceptual change in mathematics. If we are supposed not to understand certain sentences because we do not know certain mathematically necessary truths, those truths cannot be sentences. (W) preserves this distinction clearly, and it is therefore preferable to (A): since we cannot be confident now that 'Every even number is the sum of two primes' does or does not express a mathematically necessary truth, (W) implies that we do not understand the sentence.

The distinction between sentences and what they express must also be borne in mind when one turns to the consequences of Wittgenstein's claims about conceptual change. It is natural to interpret (W) as providing a necessary condition of a sentence's expressing a mathematically necessary truth. One might reason as follows. According to (W), if one does not know whether or not a certain sentence expresses a mathematically necessary truth, one does not understand the sentence. Now a sentence S expresses a given content – say, that p – in a given language L only if at least some speakers of L know that S expresses that content. If no speaker of L knows that S means that p, then S does not mean that p in L. Hence, one might argue, (W) entails that a given sentence expresses a given necessary truth only if some speakers of the relevant language know that that sentence expresses that necessary truth: S means (the mathematically necessary truth that) p in L only if some speakers of L know that S expresses p (and therefore that S expresses something necessarily true).

Appropriately refined, this necessary condition is a fair expression of Wittgenstein's views. But one must be careful to note that it is not a necessary condition of something's *being* a mathematically necessary truth; on the contrary, it is only a necessary condition of a sentence's *expressing* a mathematically necessary truth. If this distinction is conflated, the reasoning just given loses its power. There is no plausibility whatsoever in the idea that it is mathematically necessary that $5+7=12$ only if a particular community means something by '$5+7=12$'.

(W) does not, therefore, promise any account of necessity itself, in the sense in which an account must supply necessary and/or sufficient conditions. In that sense, (W) promises an account only of mathematical necessity's *expression*.

This fact about (W) points to a more general moral about Wittgenstein's later views on mathematics. Some commentators have professed to discern among those views an attempt to 'account' for logical necessity in terms of *human decision*.[3] According to these commentators, it is Wittgenstein's claim that the 'source' of logical necessity is to be found in speakers' attitudes. Now it is certainly true that Wittgenstein discussed logical necessity in his later work: (W) itself shows that, for Wittgenstein says that he sees no essential difference between logical and mathematical necessity (*RFM* I/5). But as we have just seen, (W) offers no 'account' of logical necessity itself, in the sense that it offers no necessary and sufficient conditions for something's being logically necessary. And there is a quite general reason for thinking that it is not likely that Wittgenstein *ever* attempted to offer such an account in terms of human decision. Any such account would have to hold that had certain human decisions not been made, it would not have been logically necessary that $5+7=12$ (to put it crudely). But this is tantamount to denying that it *is* logically necessary that $5+7=12$. It is plainly logically contingent that human beings make the decisions that they do make. Hence, on the suggested account, it is logically contingent that it be logically necessary that $5+7=12$. But it is definitive of logical necessity that it apply as a matter of logical necessity: if it is logically necessary that p, then it is logically necessary that it be logically necessary that p. So the necessity of $5+7=12$ depends on human decisions only if it is not logical necessity.

There is no good reason for supposing that Wittgenstein could have overlooked this point, or denied it. It depends only on the kind of reasoning invoked above in connection with (A), together with the assumption that if it is logically necessary that p, this itself holds as a matter of logical necessity. Neither of these seems disputable.

To say this is not, I should stress, to say that there is no sense of 'account' in which Wittgenstein attempted to offer an account of logical necessity itself. My point is only that he did not offer an account which makes human decision a necessary condition of something's being mathematically true. This leaves open a number of alternatives, providing that one is prepared to countenance philosophical accounts of concepts that do not proceed be retailing necessary and sufficient conditions of the application of those concepts. I make this point because it is clear that (W) itself depends on *some* general reflections aimed at establishing the existence of mathematically necessary truths. For it is a presupposition of (W) that there *are* mathematically necessary truths, and this presupposition is not beyond dispute. On the contrary, many writers (of whom the most notable contemporary example is Quine) have endorsed an empiricist or naturalist view of mathematics, on which mathematical truths are not necessary in any very interesting sense. According to these writers, '5 + 7 = 12' expresses a truth to which we are very firmly attached, but this truth is not one that could not possibly have been false. Any full defence of (W) would therefore have to provide some argument against these empiricist or naturalist views of mathematics, and this argument would certainly have to 'explain', in some sense, logical necessity itself.

Wittgenstein does not overlook this point; the *Remarks on the Foundations of Mathematics* contains sustained and powerful criticism of empiricist/naturalist views of mathematics. What is more, this criticism appeals to human decision. But this criticism is a presupposition of (W) rather than a part of the argument for (W) itself. The argument proper begins with the assumption that there are mathematically necessary truths; and it is this argument that demands our attention now.

III

My aim in this section will be to provide a general statement of the argument that led Wittgenstein to subscribe to (W). In the next section, I shall consider some likely objections to the argument.

I shall take as my point of departure *RFM* IV/29:

> So much is clear: when someone says, 'If you follow the *rule*, it *must* be like this', he has not any *clear* concept of what experience would correspond to the opposite.
>
> Or again: he has not any clear concept of what it would be like for it to be otherwise. And this is very important.

Why does Wittgenstein say that anyone who declares, 'it *must* be like this' – presumably, that a given truth holds of mathematical necessity – has no clear concept of 'what it would be like for it to be otherwise' – presumably, of what it would be for that truth not to hold? For example, one supposes that it is mathematically necessary that 5 + 7 = 12. Why should one conclude that one has no clear concept of what it would be for $5+7$ not to equal 12? An obvious answer is this: in order to have a clear concept, one must have a consistent concept. But if it is logically necessary that $5+7=12$, then it is inconsistent to suppose that $5+7$ should not equal 12, and therefore one can have no clear concept of what it would be for $5+7$ not to equal 12. More generally, if it is logically necessary that p, one cannot have a clear concept of the circumstances under which not-p, because it is inconsistent to suppose that not-p.

It may seem that this interpretation makes sense of Wittgenstein's remark only by making it trivial. Why should anyone think such a piece of reasoning 'very important'? The answer is that this reasoning suggests an argument for (W). Suppose that one wished to deny (W), on (for example) the ground that we now understand 'Every even number is the sum of two primes', though we do not know whether it expresses a mathematically necessary truth or a mathematically necessary falsehood. Then one is bound to suppose that we now have a clear concept of what it would be for every even number to be the sum of two primes. Yet *RFM* IV/29, interpreted in the way that I suggested, puts pressure on the idea that we do now possess such a concept. For the passage suggests that if one does not known whether or not it is consistent to suppose that every even number should be the sum of two primes, one cannot claim to possess a clear concept of what it would be for every even number to be the sum of two primes. A clear concept, it was said, must be a consistent one; yet prior to grasping whether or not it is necessary that p, one cannot claim to know whether it is consistent to suppose that p. How, then, can one claim to possess a clear concept of what it would be for p to be true?

It begins to become clearer, now, why *RFM* IV/29 seemed 'very important' to Wittgenstein. For it promises nothing less than a completely general argument for (W), and hence for Wittgenstein's ideas about conceptual change. Let me now try to spell out this promise more fully. It is best to conceive Wittgenstein's argument as proceeding by four stages:

(1) To possess a clear concept of what it would be for a certain situation to hold is to possess a consistent concept. Thus, to possess a clear concept of what it would be for some swans to be black is to possess a consistent concept of what it would be for some swans to be black. A 'concept' that is not consistent cannot be a clear concept; indeed, it is hardly a concept at all. Do we have any concept of what it

would be for something to be a round square?

The passage from *PI* I/517 that I quoted in I above suggests a different version of fundamentally the same point. To possess a clear concept of what it would be for a certain situation to hold is to be able to *conceive of* or *imagine* what it would be for that situation to hold. 'Concept' is, after all, closely linked to 'conceive', both etymologically and semantically, so closely that it is difficult to grasp what could be meant by describing someone as possessing a clear concept of what he cannot conceive. How could someone have a clear concept of what it would be for some swans to be black, unless he could conceive of what it would be for some swans to be black? Insofar as 'imagine' is taken to carry the same weight as 'conceive', the same connection can be made out between possession of a clear concept and a certain imaginative ability. If a speaker cannot imagine what it would be for some swans to be black, it is hard to see how he can be credited with a clear concept of what it would be for some swans to be black.

It should be noted that these points do not require one to regard imagining or conceiving as a matter of entertaining any 'private mental images'. Imagining or conceiving may here be viewed as entirely 'public' activities; *inter alia*, such activities as drawing *consistent representations*, or writing down *consistent descriptions* of what is imagined or conceived.

(2) In order to understand the sentence 'Some swans are black', one must possess either a clear concept of what it would be for some swans to be black, or at least a clear concept of what it would be for all swans not to be black. More generally, a speaker understands a sentence S only if, for some sentential content p, he knows that S means that p, and he has either a clear concept of what it would be for p to obtain, or a clear concept of what it would be for not-p to obtain.

This claim can be accepted on its own merits; but it is worth noting that it can be derived from more general points as well. It has become a philosophical commonplace to say that one understands a sentence S if and only if one knows the truth-conditions of S. Now whatever one thinks of this saying, one must agree that it can seem plausible only if knowledge of the truth-conditions of S is held to require some ability to imagine or conceive of what it would be for those conditions to obtain. If I cannot conceive of or imagine what it would be for some swans to be black, then my 'knowledge' that 'some swans are black' is true if and only if some swans are black does not amount to much.

More generally, knowing that S is true if and only if p amounts to understanding S only if such knowledge is held to include the ability to imagine or conceive of what it would be for p to obtain. Yet if that is right, I cannot understand S (i.e., know that it is true if and only if p, where in fact this is so) unless I have a clear concept of what it would be for p to hold.

Note that this reasoning does not depend on any 'realist' construction of the concept of truth. An analogous point can be made even if one wishes to insist (as Michael Dummett does) that understanding a sentence S consists in knowledge of its truth-conditions only insofar as those truth-conditions are *effectively decidable* ones – in mathematics, its *proof-conditions*. Once again, it seems fair to require that a mastery of proof-conditions involve the possession of the ability to imagine or conceive of what it would be for those conditions to obtain. If understanding 'Every even number is the sum of two primes' is taken to consist in knowing what it would be for that sentence to express something proved, knowing this must be taken to involve being able to imagine or conceive of what it would be to have a proof that every even number is the sum of two primes.

(3) One can possess no clear concept of what it would be for a logically necessary falsehood to be true. Any logically necessary falsehood is inconsistent; given that it is logically necessary that $5+7 \neq 13$, it is inconsistent to suppose that $5+7=13$. Or again, logically necessary falsehoods are inconceivable or unimaginable; given that it is logically necessary that $5+7 \neq 13$, it is inconceivable or unimaginable that $5+7=13$. So much is definitive of logical necessity: what is logically necessarily false is what cannot be conceived or imagined. To suppose otherwise is to displace logical necessity from its role as the *ruling* sort of necessity; and that is to deny that it is *logical* necessity at all. The same point holds for mathematical necessity; again, one should bear in mind that for Wittgenstein there is no essential difference between the two.

Here too the same ideas hold good even if they are put in terms of proof. If it is logically necessary that there be no greatest prime number, then it is inconsistent to suppose that one should have a proof that there is a greatest prime number. It is not just contingent that no proof is available; on the contrary, it is a matter of mathematical or logical necessity. Or again, it is inconceivable or unimaginable that one should have a proof that there is a greatest prime. Assuming that there really is no greatest prime, no such proof can be imagined or conceived of. One can provide no coherent representation or description of such a proof, for otherwise the proof would be at least logically possible.

(4) (1)–(3) supply the premisses; it remains now only to draw the conclusion, i.e. the claim (W). If one does not know whether 'Every even number is the sum of two primes' expresses a necessary truth, then, by (3), one does not know whether or not it is consistent to suppose that every even number is the sum of two primes, or to suppose that one has a proof that every even number is the sum of two primes; and, by the same token, one does not know whether it is consistent to suppose that not every even number is the sum of two primes, or to suppose that one has a proof that some number is not the sum of two primes. Hence, by (1), one cannot possess a clear concept of what it would be for every even number to be the sum of two primes, or a clear concept of what it would be for some even number not to be the sum of two primes. And hence, by (2), one cannot understand 'Every even number is the sum of two primes'. Or again, if one does not know whether 'Every even number is the sum of two primes' expresses a necessary truth, then, by (3), one is not capable of imagining what it would be for what the sentence expresses to be true, nor is one capable of conceiving of it; and one is no more capable of imagining or conceiving of what it would be for it to be proved. Hence again, by (1), one must lack a clear concept of what it would be for what 'Every even number is the sum of two primes' expresses to be true, and a clear concept of what it would be for what it expresses to be false; and hence (by (2)) one cannot understand the sentence 'Every even number is the sum of two primes'.

This, then, is what I take to be the substance of Wittgenstein's argument for (W). In a moment, I shall consider some likely objections to the argument; but before I do so, let me revert briefly to the distinction between talk of truth-conditions and talk of proof-conditions. I tried to show that the argument is insensitive to this distinction, in the sense that it goes through whether one construes an understanding of a sentence S as residing in a grasp of the conditions under which S would be true or as residing in a grasp of the conditions under which S would be proved. I did so in order to show that the argument is as effective against 'anti-realist' views of mathematics (e.g. Intuitionism) as it is against 'realist' views (e.g. Platonism). But it is worth stressing that the argument does not *prevent* Wittgenstein from expressing some sympathy with 'anti-realist' views, provided that the motivation for his sympathy springs from another source. I make this point partly because it is plausible to suppose that Wittgenstein did entertain some such anti-realist sympathies, but partly also because it is in any case worth stressing that *many* kinds of considerations inform Wittgenstein's later philosophy of mathematics. There is a tendency among some commentators to assume that there is just one fundamental theme in that philosophy (perhaps a 'conventionalist' view of necessity). This assumption is misleading; Wittgenstein's later views on mathematics are clearly plural, and his ideas about conceptual change constitute just one of these plural views.

IV

I turn now to some likely objections to the argument just sketched on behalf of (W). Naturally, I shall have to be selective here; I do not have space to give due attention to all the objections that might be raised. In particular, I shall assume that it will be generally agreed that there is *a* sense of 'clear concept' in which the second premiss of the argument is true, and therefore *a* sense of 'conceive' or 'imagine' in which it is fair to demand of anyone who understands a sentence S that he be able either to conceive of or imagine the conditions under which what S expresses would be true, or to conceive of or imagine the conditions under which what S expresses would be false. Thus, I shall take it to be uncontentious that there is a sense in which someone who understands, say, '5+7=12', must possess a clear concept of (or be able to conceive of or imagine) either what it would be for 5+7 to equal 12, or what it would be for 5+7 not to equal 12. This is, after all, a fairly weak constraint on understanding, because it is disjunctive. In order to satisfy it, one need only have either a clear concept of what it would be for a certain situation to hold, or a clear concept of what it would be for a certain situation not to hold. Stronger constraints have been put forward; for example, some writers have imposed a conjunctive constraint on understanding, requiring anyone who understands a sentence to know *both* the conditions under which it would be true *and* the conditions under which it would be false. Wittgenstein himself imposed such a constraint in the *Tractatus*, arguing that both sentences expressing necessary truths and sentences expressing necessary falsehoods are senseless. There is some evidence that he adhered to this conception at least part of the time in his later work on mathematics. But the passages cited above from *PI* I/517 and *RFM* VI/13 show that he certainly did not always do so. If there is such a thing as 'understanding' a mathematical question or 'knowing what Fermat's Last Theorem says', there must be a sense of 'sense' in which mathematical sentences are not senseless. Such a sense, I take it, is captured roughly by the weak disjunctive constraint.

To assume that this constraint will be found acceptable is not, however, to assume that the argument in which it figures will command assent. On the contrary, it will, I suspect, seem exceedingly natural to say that although there is a sense of 'clear concept' (and so of 'conceive of' or 'imagine') in which the second premiss of the argument is true, this is not a sense in which the third premiss is true. According to the third premiss, one cannot possess a clear concept of what it would be for a necessary falsehood to be true; for example, one cannot possess a clear concept of what it would be for $5+7$ not to equal 12. This claim, it might be argued, is simply false, if 'clear concept' is understood in the manner of the second premiss: in that sense of 'clear concept', one *can* form a clear concept of what it would be for a necessary falsehood to be true. Hence (it will be said) Wittgenstein's argument does not go through; we can after all understand 'Every even number is the sum of two primes', though we do not know whether or not it expresses a necessary truth.

Such a line of thought can seem overwhelmingly attractive; it can seem just obvious that we are now able to 'conceive' (in the sense relevant to understanding) of what it would be for certain undecided mathematical sentences to be true. But if this line of thought is to be evaluated soberly, certain considerations should be borne in mind.

In the first place, it is crucial to grasp that what is at stake is a speaker's ability to conceive of or imagine or represent consistently what it would *be* for certain situations to hold, and not simply what it would be *like* if certain situations held. There is one sense in which we can now imagine what it would be *like* if Goldbach's Conjecture were true, or what it would be *like* to have a proof of the Conjecture. For we can imagine numerous proofs by induction, and numerous proofs involving prime numbers and even numbers. But of course, knowing what it would be *like*, in this sense, for 'Every even number is the sum of two primes' to express a necessary truth, does not yet qualify as an understanding of 'Every even number is the sum of two primes'. My ability to construct a proof that what 'Every even number is the sum of two odd numbers' expresses is a necessary truth hardly qualifies as an understanding of Goldbach's Conjecture. Nor, more generally, does my knowledge of the meaning of numerous sentences analogous to 'Every even number is the sum of two primes' constitute an understanding of that sentence. This independence is registered in the truism that it can never follow that a given sentence has a given meaning solely from the fact that any other sentences have any other meanings. A great deal more than stipulation of *sentence*-meaning is required. Wittgenstein makes these points time and again. The larger context of the passage I cited above from *RFM* VI/13 runs, for example, as follows:

> Mathematicians are not *completely* blank when they are confronted by [Fermat's Last Theorem]. . . . But, if I am to know what a proposition like Fermat's Last Theorem says, must I not know what the criterion is, for the proposition to be true? I am of course acquainted with criteria for the truth of similar propositions, but not with any criterion for the truth of this proposition.

Compare also *RFM* V/12:

> Suppose I were to ask: what is meant by saying, 'the pattern . . . occurs in this expansion'? The reply would be: 'you surely *know* what it means. It occurs as the pattern . . . in fact occurs in the expansion.' – So is *that* the way it occurs? But *what way* is that?
>
> Imagine it were said: 'Either it occurs in that way, or it does not occur in that way'!
>
> 'But don't you really understand what is meant?' – But may I not believe I understand it, and be wrong? –
>
> For how do I know what it means to say: the pattern . . . occurs in the expansion? Surely by way of examples – which show me what it is like for. . . . But these examples do not show me what it is like for this pattern to occur in the expansion!

The force of these points is in no way diluted by the fact that one may, for example, be able to translate 'Every even number is the sum of two primes' into French. For one can translate one sentence into another without having a clear idea of what either sentence means. By the same token, one can say that 'prime number' in Goldbach's Conjecture means what it means in the sentence '17 is a prime number' without having a clear idea of what either sentence means. Knowledge of the meanings of certain sentences analogous to 'Every even number is the sum of two primes' plus knowledge of some translation-rules does not, therefore, constitute knowledge of the meaning of the sentence itself. For this reason, it is not enough that one be able to point to proofs of claims analogous to Goldbach's Conjecture; one must claim that one is able to conceive of what it would be for the Conjecture itself to be true.

But now, what if exactly that claim is made? What is Wittgenstein to say, if someone claims that he *can* imagine what it would be for Goldbach's Conjecture itself to be true? I think that Wittgenstein's answer must be (characteristically) another question: What are the relevant standards of conceivability? If it is held that there is a real sense of 'conceive' in which one can conceive of what it would be for Goldbach's Conjecture to be true (and a real sense of 'consistent' in which one can possess a consistent concept of what it would be for the Conjecture to be true), standards must be laid down. It will not do to say that just any concept is clear, or just any situation is conceivable; if the words 'conceive', 'consistent', 'imagine', etc. are not to be deprived of meaning, they must not apply in too many cases. What, then, are the limits?

This question is not an easy one. For example, it will not do to reply by appealing to *epistemic* senses for 'conceive'. There is one obvious way in which it is now conceivable that Goldbach's Conjecture should be true, and so a way in which it is possible to conceive of what it would be for the Conjecture to be true: for, if I wish to convey that I do not *know* whether the Conjecture is true, one perfectly good way to do so is by saying, 'It is conceivable that the Conjecture should be true'. Such a use of 'conceive' is certainly natural enough; so are analogous uses of 'may', and 'could'. 'For all I know, I could be wrong' (and perhaps also: 'It's consistent to suppose that I am wrong'). But these epistemic possibilities cannot be what one has in mind if one agrees – as, I am assuming, one will agree – that understanding a sentence S depends upon the ability to conceive of what it would be for what S expresses to be true (or false). So much becomes clear when one reflects that if the epistemic sense of 'conceive', 'imagine', etc. *were* what one had in mind, it would follow that we could come to know that what an *arbitrary* sentence expresses is true only at the expense of effecting a change of meaning in the relevant sentence. If there is a sense of 'conceive' in which my willingness to say, 'I don't know whether p', commits me to saying, 'It is conceivable that p', then my willingness to say, 'I know that p' commits me to saying, in this sense, 'It is inconceivable that not-p', as any epistemological skeptic will swiftly remind us. But if that is right – if any passage from ignorance to knowledge must involve a change in what one can conceive, in this sense – then it follows that I can come to grasp that what 'the cat is on the mat' says is true only by changing the meaning that I attach to 'the cat is on the mat'. Beforehand, I could 'conceive' of the conditions under which that sentence would say something false; now, I admit no such conditions. And this will hold quite generally, for any sentence at all. But now, surely this view is no more attractive than Wittgenstein's. Indeed, if anything it must seem *less* attractive. On Wittgenstein's view, conceptual change is required only when one comes to grasp a new *necessary* truth. On the current view, by contrast, *any* acquisition of knowledge must involve conceptual change.

Appeals to an epistemic sense of 'conceive' do not, therefore, look promising. If my uncertainty about whether p is taken to constitute the ability to 'conceive' of what it would be for p to obtain, it cannot be taken to constitute my understanding of anything. This, surely, is in any case the natural view; presumably only reason why I might not know whether a sentence expresses a truth is precisely that I do not know what the sentence means.

An analogous point holds good even when one turns to more sophisticated proposals. For example, someone might argue that there is a sense in which one can 'conceive' of what it would be for an *unobvious* necessary truth – e.g. that there are no constructible heptagons – to be false, though one cannot conceive of what it would be for an *obvious* necessary truth – e.g. that there are no round squares – to be false. The suggestion would then be that it is this sense that we have in mind when we agree that understanding a sentence depends on being able to conceive of what it would be for what that sentence expresses to be true. For this reason, one might conclude, we *can* now understand 'Every even number is the sum of two primes' – for whatever else it is, Goldbach's Conjecture is not *obviously* true or false.

In effect, this suggestion is designed to meet Wittgenstein half way. It agrees with him in holding that *some* necessary truths cannot be grasped for the first time without a conceptual change, or a change in one's understanding. For it implies that anyone who comes to grasp for the first time that it is obviously necessary that e.g. $3+4=7$ must undergo a conceptual change, and therefore effect a change in the meaning that he attaches to '$3+4=7$' (assuming he attaches any meaning at all to it). But the suggestion is designed nevertheless to depart from Wittgenstein over some necessary truths; it is designed to preserve the idea that one can understand sentences expressing unobvious necessary truths or falsehoods, without knowing which. These, after all, are presumably the sentences that we want most to understand.

Unfortunately, this suggestion is not coherent. It would work only if we could guarantee ourselves a privileged access to what is and is not obvious; for only if we could be sure that Goldbach's Conjecture really was not obviously necessary would this suggestion allow us to be sure that we now possess a clear concept of what it would be for every even number to be the sum of two primes. Now in one sense it is of course true that we can be confident that the Conjecture's truth or falsity is unobvious, for in one sense what is obvious boils down to what we *find* obvious. But in this sense, the same truth may be both obvious and unobvious at the same time; it may be obvious to you that the Binomial Theorem holds, but not obvious to me. Yet the suggestion leaves no room for this sort of tolerance concerning the obvious. According to the suggestion, if it is obviously necessary that the Binomial Theorem be true, then anyone who does not grasp that it is obvious must lack the relevant concepts. Hence, the mere fact that he does not *find* the Theorem obvious does not show that it *is* not obvious. By the same token, the mere fact that we do not find the correct verdict on Goldbach's Conjecture obvious cannot, of itself, be taken to show that the verdict is not obvious. In view of this, the suggestion loses most of its appeal; for how can we now be confident that it is *not* obvious that every even number is the sum of two primes?

We have discovered, then, no good reason for supposing that there is a clear sense in which one can conceive of what it would be for an undecided mathematical claim to be true, and therefore understand it. Of course, various alternatives have not been canvassed; there remain senses of 'conceive', 'imagine' and so on in terms of which, one might argue, we can credit ourselves with the ability to understand undecided mathematical claims. But we have seen enough to suggest a general difficulty in any such argument, and I shall conclude by commenting briefly on this.

I noted in II above that Wittgenstein's argument for (W) presupposes that there are mathematically necessary truths, and therefore that empiricism or naturalism concerning mathematics is misguided. One may not endorse this presupposition; but if one does, then one is obliged to distinguish oneself from the empiricist or naturalist, when and if one departs from Wittgenstein. Yet this seems curiously difficult to do. As we have seen, the argument for (W) hinges on the idea that what is mathematically or logically impossible is also inconceivable, in the sense of 'conceivable' that is relevant to understanding. If, now, one abandons that idea, one begins to lose one's grip on mathematical or logical impossibility altogether. For what exactly does it *mean* to say, e.g., that it is logically impossible that $5+7=12$, but nevertheless it is entirely conceivable the $5+7$ should not have equalled 12 (and that one has a perfectly clear concept of what it would have been for $5+7$ not to have equalled 12, so clear that one can provide a consistent description of the relevant situation)? How can one now explain what logical necessity amounts to? What has become of the difference between necessity and contingency? The answers to these questions are by no means *obvious*. But if they are not, then one must concede that Wittgenstein is not *obviously* wrong to subscribe to (W).

V

Suppose that Wittgenstein is right, and (W) is true. Then some widely received ideas about mathematics will have to be re-examined. For example, one is inclined to regard new theorems and new proofs in mathematics as *discoveries*. The mathematician, one supposes, is engaged in a *search* which, if successful, issues in his *recognition* of mathematical truth. These idioms of search, discovery, and recognition are deeply embedded in our reflective consciousness of mathematics. But if Wittgenstein is right, these idioms are misleading. In order to search for something, one must possess a clear concept of what one seeks; in order to recognize or discover the solution to a problem, one must possess in advance a sharp idea of what such a solution would be.

According to Wittgenstein, no such prior ideas or concepts are available to the mathematician. Instead, the mathematician's results are wholly *new* concepts. Hence a different set of images is required to describe the evolution of mathematics. We must now resort to the metaphor of *invention*, viewing the mathematician as one who *decides*, rather than one who recognizes. And we must revere with a new candour the mathematician's *creativity*; as Wittgenstein put it, 'The mathematician creates *essence*' (*RFM* I/32).

It may seem that such a shift in our mode of description would threaten the *rationality* of mathematical progress. If the task of the mathematician is only to create new concepts or to decide on new meanings then, one might conclude, Wittgenstein must take the mathematician to be beyond rational criticism, for presumably one is free to adopt whatever concepts one chooses. But this conclusion would be hasty. As Wittgenstein repeatedly reminds us, we do have standards by which to criticize proposals introducing new concepts:

> [Mathematics] forms ever new rules: is always building new roads for traffic; by extending the network of old ones.
> But then doesn't it need a sanction for this? Can it extend the network *arbitrarily*? Well, I could say: a mathematician is always inventing new forms of description. Some, stimulated by practical needs, others, from aesthetic needs, – and yet others in a variety of ways. (*RFM* I/165–6)

We may criticize a proposed solution to, say, a number-theoretic problem on the grounds that endorsing it involves accepting a concept of number that is not useful for e.g. physics. Or again, we may criticize a new mathematical proposal in, say, set-theory, on aesthetic grounds, dismissing it as 'inelegant'. And there are still other possibilities, depending upon the uses to which we wish to put the concepts in questions, the needs and interests they are designed to serve.

Of course, these modes of criticism rely heavily on 'evaluative' judgements. If they are to be made effective, we must be able to secure agreement that utility for physics, elegance and so on are worth respecting. Analytic philosophy has familiarized us with the idea that such agreement is somehow less than fully rational. But it would be unwise to *assume* that Wittgenstein would endorse that idea. A better conclusion would be that one of Wittgenstein's aims, in advancing (W), was to free us from the view of rationality that forces us to regard evaluation as less than rational. One of the main props supporting that view has been the thought that mathematics affords a paradigm of inquiry almost entirely free of evaluative agreements; it is held that the mathematician is constrained solely by the inexorable demands of *consistency*. If Wittgenstein is right, that prop at any rate is insecure: the demand for consistency is in fact a plurality of demands, depending on our purposes and interests. We are no less – and no more – free in mathematics to adopt the conclusions we do than we are to endorse those purposes and interests. If we can bring ourselves to recognize this much, then we can also see how Wittgenstein may have been attempting to preserve a place for the rational assessment of human purposes and interests. Such an attempt no doubt has its risks. But they are certainly no greater than the risks involved in denying rational responsibility to mathematical endeavours.

The philosophy of mathematics since Frege has been conducted largely under the assumption that one has just two choices when it comes to assessing the general character of mathematical progress. On the one hand, one may affirm the necessity of mathematical truth, in which case one is committed to the idea that the mathematician is a kind of geographer of antecedently existing conceptual connections. On the other hand, one may deny the necessity of mathematical truth, in which case one is committed to the idea that '5+7=12' expresses only a glorified inductive generalization. Neither of these alternatives is especially attractive. The first fails to account for the fact that mathematics can yield results that are essentially *new*; if we are now committed, by the meanings we have attached to 'even number' and so on, to regarding Goldbach's Conjecture as either the expression of a necessary falsehood, or a necessary truth, then it is a mystery how a solution to the problem might prove surprising. The second alternative promises to do justice to the novelty of mathematical results – but only at the price of representing the mathematician's procedure as unduly *hasty*. If mathematical results are not necessary, should the mathematician not take to the laboratory, if he is to do his job properly? Wittgenstein's third, alternative position manages to avoid the weaknesses of these two. If the progress of mathematics involves the formation of new concepts, we can account for both the novelty and necessity of new mathematical results. To be sure, Wittgenstein's position is less *comforting* than the other two alternatives. But we have already seen that the need for comfort here may be based on a conception of security that needs re-examination.

3

Post-structuralism, Empiricism and Interpretation

Sollace Mitchell

Incontestably there is today a rift between the English and French-speaking traditions of philosophy. It is in some ways so profound that it makes translation from one philosophical language into the other look like the impossible ideal of some forgotten universalism. Imagine one of Donald Davidson's radical translators seated unobtrusively in Jacques Derrida's latest seminar, the post-structuralist vocabulary flying past him. '*Lapin*' would be the least of his problems.

Yet the two traditions do share a common interest: the question of how language bears on philosophy. Might they not, then, have something to say to one another? The enthusiasts for a reconciliation of the two schools suggest that their isolation is regrettable, that they would do better to foster more intimate contacts. Surely there is something to be said for lowering philosophical import duties. But, in the spirit of pluralism, I might point out that isolation leads to independent development, without which the issue of an exchange of ideas would have no compelling interest. If we do have something to learn from the French, or they from us, it is precisely because we have for so long gone our separate ways.

With this in mind, I propose to pinpoint the essential differences between the two traditions, which I shall broadly call analytical and post-structuralist. Both these categories subsume a number of different approaches, not all of which can be done justice by a focused discussion. Accordingly, I shall look mainly at the empiricist strands of analytical philosophy, on the one hand, and at the work of Jacques Derrida, on the other, whose methodology and view of philosophy differ most radically from that prevailing in England and America. My references to Derrida will be illustrative, not exegetical, as my aim is not so much to make his work available as to bring into clear relief the challenges which the analytical and post-structuralist tendencies present to one another. (I shall not, for example, weigh the pros and cons of Derrida's central notions, *archi-écriture* and *différance*-with-an-a.)

The aims of philosophy

In his contribution to a recent number of *Critique* devoted to 'Anglo-Saxon Philosophy', Jonathan Barnes condenses the differences between the English and French approaches into a 'vicious' *aperçu*: 'The English vice is to covet the truth while ignoring history; the French vice is to be content with the past while forgetting philosophy' ('Aristote chez les Anglophones', p. 708).

If the formula is over-simple, it nevertheless points us in the right direction. Though contemporary English-speaking philosophers are keenly aware of their special empiricist heritage, the use that is today made of inherited philosophical texts is primarily self-serving, by which I mean that a look at what a past philosopher was interested in turns out invariably to be a look at what the present philosopher is interested in, no matter what his forebear might really have intended. In some cases, the divergence is unwitting, as in Bertrand Russell's *The Philosophy of Leibniz*; in others, the writer is perfectly well aware that he is treating a modernized version of the arguments in question. The latter approach is the vogue, and is to be found in a number of recent studies, notably as expressed by Peter Strawson in *Individuals* (p. 117): 'When I allude to the system of Leibniz, I will scarcely be troubled if the doctrines I discuss are not at each point identical with the historical doctrines espoused by the philosopher called Leibniz.'[1]

Of this approach it can be said that even if we abandon the hope of recovering precisely what the author wished to say – what I shall call the *authority* of the text, that shouldn't inhibit us in our search for solutions to the questions he seems to have raised, even if we consider faulty the answers we impute to him.

The post-structuralists assume a similar posture with respect to the author of the text they seek to analyse, for they regard it as pointless to try to recapture the original intention. Indeed, it is a main tenet of Derrida's theory of writing-in-general (*archi-écriture*) that the text (or any sign) is a material trace cut off from whoever penned it; thus it must be taken at its word, as an independent discursive artifact. To some extent this allows the interpreter, or *reader*, a greater freedom. It is not, however, a licence for offering any reading that strikes one's fancy. There remains the profoundly difficult question as to what makes one interpretation authoritative, another frivolous. For a text will sanction some readings, but not all. Insofar as it utilizes particular concepts and particular logical and rhetorical structures, it calls for a response that will do justice to those features that distinguish it from other works by the same author, or from works by different authors. To this extent, at least, the analytical and post-structuralist schools are in accord: one can go only so far in attributing to a text concepts whose associated words do not explicitly appear therein.

Here is where the similarity between the two traditions ends, for the post-structuralists take as their primary object of analysis other texts, whereas the analytical philosophers, despite their focus on language, do not. The major figures of recent French thought have been almost exclusively readers of texts: Claude Lévi-Strauss – the mythological texts of non-technological cultures; Jacques Lacan – the discourse of the patient in psychoanalysis; Michel Foucault – the texts of an historical epoch; Roland Barthes – literary texts and cultural productions in general; and Derrida – other philosophers' texts (Plato, Rousseau, Hegel, Nietzsche, Husserl, Heidegger, Freud).

The motto for this approach might be taken from the epigraph to Derrida's essay on Lévi-Strauss, namely, Montaigne's dictum that 'We need to interpret interpretations more than to interpret things.' To understand what governs the way we see the world, and how our vision is metaphysically prejudiced, the post-structuralists insist on scrutinizing the text of philosophy as it has been written since the pre-Socratics. They claim that it is only within the text that we have access to the workings of our language. Meaning, on this view, is always an effect of discourse alone. And this is the assumption that underlies that particular way of reading a text which Derrida calls *deconstruction*:

> if reading must not be content with doubling the text [i.e., giving a classical commentary on what the author said], it cannot legitimately transgress the text toward something other than it, toward a referent (a reality that is metaphysical, historical, psycho-biographical, etc.) or toward a signified outside the text whose content could take place, could have taken place outside language, that is to say, in the sense we give here to the word,

outside of writing in general. . . . There is no outside-of-text [Il n'y a pas de hors-texte].
(*Of Grammatology*, E p. 158; F p. 227)

As I will show, this conception of the immanence of the text's significance is closely tied to the picture of linguistic meaning that underpins it. But before contrasting the post-structuralist theory of meaning with its analytical counterpart, let me consider a view that gives the written text a secondary status in the quest for philosophical understanding.

One reason that contemporary analytical philosophers are not often troubled about the particular historical doctrine expressed by a text, is that they are comparatively unconcerned with how their own search for solutions to philosophical problems might have been determined by the tradition they inherit. It is believed that the issues of the puzzle at hand are what they are, no matter what its derivation, and that the attempt to solve it must succeed or fail on its own account. In a sense, the outstanding questions of philosophy are independent of the various philosophers who have sought to answer them; and if the questions persist, it is simply because past treatments have been defective. Philosophical progress might more readily be made if we treat a problem area scientifically, with a common, systematic methodology and programme of research, rather than historically. Thus Michael Dummett claims that philosophy has just recently entered its maturity by taking as its central concern the formulation of a systematic theory of meaning for natural language:

> We have now reached a position where the search for such a theory of meaning can take on a genuinely scientific character; this means, in particular, that it can be carried on in such a way, not, indeed, that disputes do not arise, but that they can be resolved to the satisfaction of everyone, and, above all, that we may hope to bring the search within a finite time to a successful conclusion.
> ('Can Analytical Philosophy be Systematic?', p. 454)

As Dummett freely confesses, his opinion smacks of an optimism usually associated with the idea that we (i.e., current philosophers) survey the tradition from its historical end-point, and thereby are afforded a privileged view of the past advances (and set-backs) of philosophical progress. Dummett cannot justify this belief to the sceptic, but he holds it no less tenaciously. (There is an element of faith here. Dummett speaks of himself as a prophet insofar as he holds a brief for the systematicity of post-Fregean philosophical semantics. Hilary Putnam is more explicit: 'Belief in a true answer [to the question whether there is an ideally true conception of rationality] may be religious belief (it certainly answers the question: "What can we hope for?"); at bottom, it is my religion' (' "Si dieu est mort, alors tout est permis . . .": Réflexions sur la philosophie du langage', p. 801).)

If philosophy is, as Dummett believes, 'one – perhaps the most important – sector in the quest for truth', it is liable to make progress only because (or if) it treats of facts. That is to say, philosophizing ought to issue in a set of true propositions: declarative sentences that have been conclusively verified. These propositions may pertain to many sorts of philosophical enquiry: ethics, aesthetics, philosophy of mind, philosophy of science, political theory, and so forth. Of course, there is no guarantee that every proposition in which we (enlightened philosophers) believe will in fact be true. Analytical philosophers are divided about whether we are justified in hoping to settle all the questions that currently interest us. But they are generally agreed on one point: that we can have no hope whatsoever of deciding such questions unless we correctly grasp the meanings of the sentences expressing those propositions. For one condition of determining a proposition's truth or falsity is an understanding of the proposition itself. Without a firm grasp of the meaning, the question of factualness, or truth, doesn't get started. We might, for example, be misled into regarding as meaningful a proposition that, upon closer examination, turns out to be non-sensical, incapable of bearing any truth-value at all. How, then, shall we decide whether a proposition makes sense or not, whether we truly grasp the meanings of our expressions?

We will need a reliable theory of meaning for the language in which we couch our philosophical statements. Only thereby will we be able to assess the semantic character of the sentence: to see whether it makes sense, and if so, just what sense it makes. As such, a theory of meaning would underpin all other philosophical pursuits, and their claims would have to be measured equally against the semantic theory as against the world they address themselves to. (Naturally, different theories of meaning will yield different conclusions as to the semantic character of the sentence in question, so the systematic philosopher will be anxious to come up with the right theory – if indeed there is a single, correct theory.)

In one respect, interest in a theory of meaning for our language is the corollary of the older philosophical interest in the laws of thought. The modern and unifying feature of the various analytical schools is the conviction that we can understand the structure of thought only by analysing the structure of language, for a thought is held to be nothing but a linguistic expression. When we have understood the structure of language we will be able to see just how our thoughts stand in relation to the way things are. Language looms large on the philosophical horizon because we cannot hope for any adequate epistemology, ontology, or metaphysics without some means of assessing their constituent propositions. In a sense, then, getting it right about language is important because getting it right about the non-discursive world is important.

This attitude runs through many different schools in the analytical community. It was most baldly evident in the doctrines of logical positivism, with its verificationist theory of meaning, by means of which the positivist sought to dismiss as non-sensical any proposition whose truth could not be established by experience or logical inference. It is also quite visible in the American-based inheritors of positivism, notably Rudolf Carnap and W.V.O. Quine, both of whose philosophies are convergent with empirical methodology in the natural sciences. But it is equally present, though not so obviously, in the linguistic philosophy associated with Oxford in the forties and fifties. In fact, as far back as 1931 Gilbert Ryle wrote:

> there is after all a sense in which we can properly enquire and even say 'what it really means to say so and so'. For we can ask what is the real form of the fact recorded when this is concealed or disguised and not duly exhibited by the expression in question. And we can often succeed in stating this fact in a new form of words which does exhibit what the other failed to exhibit. And I am for the present inclined to believe that this is what philosophical analysis is, and that this is the sole and whole function of philosophy.
>
> ('Systematically Misleading Expressions', p. 61)

If Ryle's formulation is somewhat extreme, nevertheless it is similar in spirit to Dummett's contention that 'the correctness of any piece of analysis carried out in another part of philosophy cannot be fully determined until we know with reasonable certainty what form a correct theory of meaning for our language must take' ('Can Analytical Philosophy be Systematic?', p. 454).

The idea that a semantic theory is the foundation of successful philosophy in other areas is one aspect of systematicity. The other is to be found within the theory of meaning itself, which is regarded as systematic if it treats sentences as complexes constructed from a finite set of simples (or words). The theory's job is to make explicit a limited number of rules that govern the combination of the simples. These rules will comprise the language's logical grammar. By reference to that grammar any sentence can be semantically broken down into its constituent parts, each of which will belong to a certain category of expression (names, predicates, syncategoremata, etc.). The meaning of the complex will depend on the meanings of the simples out of which it is built. Our understanding of the language, or of all its propositions, will thus be no more nor less clear than our understanding of how the semantic simples come to have a sense. The general idea is that by adequately parsing our language into a set of surveyable simples (and rules for their combination) we can see how it fits into an isomorphic relation with the world. (I shall discuss the referential character of systematic theories of meaning in the following section.) Once this relation is made plain, it is thought, we will have the basic tools necessary for working our way to the end of philosophical problems that perplex us.

It is one of the identifying characteristics of post-structuralist thought that it regards as an anathema such devotion to the systematic, especially in the first of its two aspects. For one, it treats the idea of philosophical progress with the utmost suspicion. The questions of philosophy are posable, considerable, but not answerable: we can respond to them, but without thereby laying them to rest. (Says Derrida: 'When I attempt to decipher a text, I do not constantly wonder whether I will end up by answering with a categorical *yes* or *no*, as is done in France during specific eras in history, and in general on Sundays' ('Positions', E p. 40; F p. 110).) Progress, on this quite different view, consists of a progression of interpretations. Thus the text is left free to play out its significance in the hands of different readers.

Indeed, the written text is regarded as having a certain autonomy, one that speech was thought never to attain. Classically, the spoken word was seen as the primary bearer of meaning; the written word was treated as a means of recording, or representing, speech, and so was viewed as a derivative, secondary kind of sign. The spoken word gained its meaning through its relation to thought, as a palpable and public garment for what was impalpable and private. (No one ever found it necessary to ask how thoughts got *their* meaning.) In the seventeenth century, these mental semantic units were commonly called 'ideas', for example by John Locke, who maintained that 'The use of words is to be the sensible marks of ideas; and the ideas they stand for are their proper and immediate signification.'

Locke's theory is a species of conceptualism, the view that words are endowed with meaning because ideas are immediately *present* to them. This theory fosters the notion that the very utterance of the word guarantees it a meaning, and can lead to the mistaken belief that meaning subsists in the mind independently of the words that serve as its expressive foundation. (This is a natural mistake to make at first glance. We often say such things as, 'I have the thought in my head even before I say the words'.) The mental content, or spirit, that is taken to be present somehow in the word may be called, after the Greeks, *logos*, a kind of divinely generated and transcendental semantic presence.

Derrida argues that in the Western tradition of thinking about language, from the pre-Socratics right up to Heidegger, every theory of meaning, covertly or not, makes appeal to this notion of *logos*. It is just this doctrine of meaning, as a presence living in the word, that Derrida attacks, calling it logocentric. As will be seen, Derrida does not confine his critique of what he calls 'the metaphysics of presence' to conceptualism; he regards theories that base meaning on the relation of a word to the thing it refers to as equally logocentric, since they too, as he claims, rely on the notion of the thing somehow being made present to the word.

Against all this, Derrida poses the fact of writing, which more clearly challenges the conception of meaning as the presence, for example, of an original intention that supposedly inhabits the word. What about the written text, which exists independently, cut off from any guarantee of meaning? In writing, the sign's 'original meaning' is detached from it to the degree that the text detaches itself from its author, or loses its authority. It is this loss (which Derrida argues to be a necessary one) that allows for the subsequent intervention of the reader, and which makes textual interpretation so difficult. Meaning is always at risk.

By reversing the emphasis on the spoken and written signs, Derrida has not substituted some other semantic principle in place of *logos*; rather, he has shifted the focus from meaning as a product of intention (*'vouloir-dire'*) to meaning as a product of convention. As I will show in the following section, this step brings him appreciably nearer to a systematic theory of language. For the moment, I will note that even if writing assumes a primary importance in semantic questions, there remains a problem about the presence of the speaker as the intentional agent who stands behind the discourse. Whether it is written or spoken, we must still account for how a sign (as one sort of object among others) comes to mean something.

Once Derrida emphasizes the written (or 'grammatological') nature of the sign, he can return to speech and point out the ways in which it too is cut off from any immediately present fund of content. For a spoken sign is no less a material trace than a written one – it just doesn't last as long. As part of a text, the aural mark is in one respect inscribed; it is a form of writing-in-general. The sound that instantiates the spoken word does not itself contain any meaning. We are misled if we are inclined to think there is present in speech anything more than the sound of the voice. We are entitled to wonder equally about the meaning of spoken as of written signs, since even the opportunity to ask the speaker what he means gives us no assurance that the words will be properly or coherently glossed. Once the word leaves the mouth it stands as independently as the sign inscribed on the page. The speaker has no more – nor less – right to determine the sense of his words (which are no longer strictly *his*) than the hearer. He can try to clarify his utterance, but he cannot rob it of the sense it has in virtue of belonging to a given language. Further, there are many times when the hearer is in a better position to judge the meaning of the spoken words than the speaker himself. Someone imperfectly in command of the language may not realize quite what he has just said. Even a competent speaker doesn't always know precisely what the full sense of his words is.

If, as Derrida claims, anything that qualifies as a sign is necessarily cut off from any semantic source, then to understand it we will have to read significance into it. This will hold true no less of the speaker (or writer) than of the hearer (or reader). (If I am to be counted a competent speaker I must at least be able to grasp the meaning of the words I utter – whether it be at the moment of utterance or many days later, as when I pore over old notes.)

But reading as Derrida understands it is not a task of restoring to the text the vitality of some original meaning. The yearning for a 'true' meaning must be thwarted as soon as the sign is let loose. A text may inspire an unending spiral of interpretations, but the point is not to capture what the author intended, but instead what the words themselves will support. Unlike traditional hermeneutics (but similar to Heidegger's interest in the *Dasein* quality of language), Derrida's deconstructive readings don't hanker after what the author wished to say, but after what the *text* wishes to say (and often, oddly enough, given Derrida's anti-intentionalism, after what the author wished *not* to say). One deconstruction will itself, of course, always be open to a further deconstruction: there is no correct or final reading.

Derrida describes the two sorts of interpretation while affirming his commitment to criticize the metaphysical notion of meaning as a species of presence inhering in the sign:

> The one seeks to decipher, dreams of deciphering a truth or an origin which escapes play and the order of the sign, and which lives the necessity of interpretation as an exile. The other, which is no longer turned toward the origin, affirms play and tries to pass beyond man and humanism, . . . that being who, throughout the history of metaphysics . . . has dreamed of full presence, the reassuring foundation, the origin and end of play.
> ('Structure, Sign and Play', E p. 292; F p. 427)

Because Derrida's deconstructive method is distinct from the more traditional enterprise of hermeneutics, I shall call his style of philosophy *lectural*, as opposed to analytical or interpretative.

The lectural approach is not content to search for the mere 'meaning' of the text, what we can call its *signified*. Rather, the reading attends to the text's formal character, to the actual words and turns of phrase out of which it is constructed, what we may call its *signifiers*. For this reason an important focus of deconstructive readings is the style of the discourse: the effect produced by the particular choice of expressive vehicle that is made within each text. Derrida insists that the signified cannot be separated from the signifier.

In consequence, any adequate reading of a text must take into account the manner in which what the text says is a product of how it is said. As such, lecturalism naturally lends itself to literary criticism.[2] The mistake, according to Derrida, is to think that there is a sharp division between what is philosophical and what is literary. For instance, a philosophical text is just as importantly informed by a particular style or rhetorical strategy as is a literary text. (Think of the styles we associate with different German-speaking philosophers: Kant, Hegel, Nietzsche, Heidegger, Wittgenstein. Perhaps the mode of expression is peculiar to what is expressed in those texts. Indeed, what is expressed is in part dependent on that mode of expression.)

Derrida insists that we cannot consider the philosopher's arguments in isolation from the discursive idiosyncrasies of the text:

> Even if there is never a pure signified, there are different relationships as to that which, from the signifier, *is presented* as the irreducible stratum of the signified. For example, the philosophical text, although it is in fact always written, includes precisely as its philosophical specificity, the project of effacing itself before the signified content which it transports and in general teaches.
>
> (*Of Grammatology*, E p. 160; F p. 229)

Philosophy, then, might be distinguished from literature according to the attitude the text seems to exhibit toward its form of expression. If the text calls attention to its form, treats it as being equally pertinent to the overall semantic effect as its content, it would qualify as literary. If, however, it seeks to make its form transparent and present its content directly, for consideration on its own, then it would qualify as philosophical. But for all its transparency, the philosophical text retains a determinate style, one that represents itself as making no essential reference to its expressive vehicle.

In this respect, it is argued, philosophical discourse is ingenuous – at least insofar as it aims to carry us beyond itself into a realm of pure argument or thesis. Derrida likens this to the notion of the non-linguistic idea, a concept that makes unconscious appeal to a 'transcendental signified'. If philosophizing is always to consist in a desire to carry us to Truth (in the absolutist, Hegelian sense of Spirit coming to itself), then Derrida's project is to jump outside philosophy, if possible, in order to see more clearly the assumptions with which it operates. For if we continue to work within the Western metaphysical tradition (as Derrida so casually refers to it), to regard philosophy as 'the most important sector in the quest for truth', we shall only prolong our blindness to the basis of that metaphysics: 'What I want to emphasize is that the passage beyond philosophy does not consist in turning the page of philosophy (which usually amounts to philosophizing badly), but in continuing to read philosophers *in a certain way* ('Structure, Sign and Play', E p. 288; F pp. 421–2).

In sum, the aim in deconstructing philosophical texts is twofold: 1) to expose their implicit reliance on certain metaphysical doctrines; and 2) to see how philosophy works as a mode of linguistic discourse, much as any other kind of discourse with a particular stylistic character (literary, political, mercantile, etc.).

Evidently there is no question of decidability here, the more so because the object of analysis is considered to be inexhaustible. It seems that the text cannot be limited to a single interpretation. A particular reading (whether by the author, as an explanation, or by the critic) sets to work but one among many possible discourses that constitute the text's potential to, as it were, rewrite itself. Derrida explains:

> I call by the name *discourse* the current, living, conscious *representation* of a text within the experience of the person who writes or reads it, . . . the text constantly goes beyond this representation by the entire system of its resources and its own laws. . . .
> (*Of Grammatology*, E p. 101; F p. 149)

Such a discourse does not deplete the *text* because, contrary to the text's 'free-play', a particular discourse enshrines the reader's attempts to confer or impose a signified upon the signifiers confronting him:

> this task of deconstruction cannot be a purely 'theoretical' or 'conceptual' or 'discursive' one; I mean the working of a discourse governed entirely by essence, meaning, truth, intention, consciousness, ideality, etc. What I call *text* is also what 'in

practice' inscribes and extends beyond the limits of such a discourse. There is such a general text wherever (i.e., everywhere) this discourse and its order (essence, meaning, truth, intention, consciousness, identity, etc.) are exceeded, i.e., wherever their occurrence is reset in the position of a mark within a chain of signifiers, and it is the structurally necessary illusion of that discourse to want and to believe that it governs that chain. ('Positions', E p. 43; F p. 116)

What is it for the 'general text' to exceed the confines of discourse? Here the claim is not merely that the text is more than the whole of its content. Rather, the text is being generalized to the point where it covers what is traditionally thought of as both the discursive and non-discursive realms. Bluntly, the claim is that the world, under Western eyes, is the general text. Such is the upshot of Derrida's insistence that reading 'cannot legitimately transgress the text toward something other than it'. Wherever language, wherever thought itself intervenes in our world, there is nothing but text (*'Il n'y a pas de hors-texte'*). Language is always at work in our reflection on the world, and there is no going beyond it, directly to a world of language-independent things, or to a metaphysical world of pure content.

In this respect, Derrida's position is recognizably Kantian. First, because he argues (more radically than Kant) that language is the limit of the world. Our concepts, as the objects of our judgements, are bounded by what is given to us in the text. We cannot, by means of reasoning, conclude to what lies beyond the text. Derrida further risks the view, unwarranted according to Kant, that there is no *logos* or divine presence that transcends our inscripted world. The second resemblance lies in Derrida's admission that there may be worldly things-in-themselves. Like Kant, he considers that, insofar as these things are available to thought, they are objects whose phenomenal aspect is constructed within the general text. Our world, says Derrida, consists of what can be framed within our language. Not that there is *nothing* beyond the text – the world is out there; but that there is no outside-of-text which figures in our understanding of our propositions.

Here we begin to see the glimmerings of idealism. Though he subscribes to a boundary-theory of language and knowledge (the limit of language is the limit of the knowable world), Derrida differs from, say, the verificationists in his denial that the category of experience figures in our grasp of the meanings of our words. Neither is he a realist, for he counts as non-sensical the claim that objects (e.g., the referents of our expressions) exist independently of our ability to seize them within the text.

I should make it clear that Derrida himself nowhere explicitly endorses the view of the philosophical analysandum that I have ascribed to him. But it is the only coherent view on the matter that can be extracted from his writings. And it is clearly at odds with the attitudes prevailing in the systematic strands of the analytical tradition, whose fundamental empiricism is most apparent in its theories of meaning. In Anglo-American eyes the post-structuralist theory of meaning in general (and the implicit Derridean theory in particular) will look thoroughly idealist. Although Derrida would protest, since he regards idealism as the most obvious form of logocentrism, there is something to be said for classifying his conception of linguistic meaning as idealist – at least insofar as it eschews appeal to any relation of sign to thing in favour of a signified produced entirely within a matrix of signifiers.

Each of the two meta-philosophical views I have been considering, the analytical and the lectural, are heavily influenced by the semantic theories that are associated with them, though it would be difficult to say which level determines which. The motivation for making language one's central object of philosophical interest may no more dictate one's theory of meaning than one's theory will guide one's conception of the philosophical enterprise in general. But there can be no doubt that the two are interdependent, and by contrasting analytical with post-structuralist semantics we will see more clearly what is at stake in the opposition of the two systems of philosophy.

Philosophy and meaning

The contrasting aims of analytical empiricism and post-structuralism are reflected in their semantic theories, which I shall call empiricist and idealist. By 'empiricist theory of meaning' I mean the view that semantic value is produced in the relation holding between sign and thing (word and object): the value of the word is the object to which it refers (or the contribution it makes to a sentence whose reference is a particular truth-value). By 'idealist theory of meaning' I mean the view that semantic value is produced in the relation holding between sign and concept. The former relation, for obvious reasons, is *referential*, and holds between two distinct realms, the linguistic and the objective. The latter relation is, as I shall argue, *metaphorical*, and holds within an immanent linguistic realm.

Here, then, in outline form, are the empiricist and idealist theories:

A referential theory of meaning is today invariably a neo-Fregean theory, for it was Frege who considered reference to consist of a relation between word and object. If, for example, a noun is abstract rather than concrete (e.g., 'number' as opposed to 'tiger') then its referent is an existing abstract object rather than a concrete object. Frege's realism, however, is foremost an epistemological rather than an ontological thesis, for he was concerned not so much to establish the reality of a thought (that which is expressed by a complete declarative sentence) as its objectivity, thereby explaining why it is equally available to whoever can grasp the meaning of the sentence. In fact, according to Frege, we do not have direct knowledge of an object; rather, we grasp something about that object through the medium of a proposition. When we know something about an object, we know a proposition about that object. Furthermore, we cannot ask after the referent of a word in isolation from the role it plays in a proposition. This is one of the upshots of Frege's doctrine that only in the context of a sentence does a word have a reference. The proposition, then, not the single word, is regarded as having semantic primacy.

Nevertheless, though much of our knowledge is propositional, the meaning of the individual word consists in the directions it gives us for determining what particular object it latches onto in the non-discursive world. (This, anyway, is the view entailed by Frege's distinction between the sense and the reference of a word. Today, however, many American semanticists dispense with this reference-presenting character and appeal directly to the referent itself in fixing a word's content. But I think this idea creates more problems than it solves.)

Thus when a speaker knows the meaning of a word, he knows at least two distinct but related things: the reference of the word (the referent of the name or the extension of the predicate); and how to use the word correctly in framing propositions about the world. In this respect, although a given theory of meaning will imply certain ontological and metaphysical conclusions, its fundamental task is often taken to be an epistemological one: to give the necessary and sufficient conditions of a knowledge whose possession would confer on the speaker (or translator) a grasp of the meaning of the word (or language) in question. (Just how rich the specification of knowledge should be, i.e., whether the theory should make explicit a rule implicitly grasped by the native speaker, is a matter of debate, principally between Michael Dummett, who favours a rich theory, and Donald Davidson and John McDowell, who favour an austere one.[3])

A referential theory, whether strictly Fregean or not, entails that the object of semantic knowledge (the bearer of the name) is made present to the knowing subject through the agency of the proposition. When we know something, that knowledge consists in seizing the object by its semantic handle. We ought therefore to distinguish in the referential theory between realism and objectivism. According to realism, objects of propositional knowledge (including abstract objects, such as truth-values) exist independently of the knowing subject and his ability to grasp the object through experience or inference. Light-waves, for example, exist whether they are seen or not. Similarly, the truth-value of a sentence that is for us effectively undecidable (such as the negation of an existential quantification), is thought to exist nevertheless. (Realism is based on the principle of bivalence, which says that every proposition is either true or false. I leave out of account a strain of referential theory called 'anti-realist', where the existence of truth-values is tied to the speaker's ability to verify the proposition.)

Whereas realism has an ontological emphasis, objectivism has an epistemological one. To know the meaning of a word is to have knowledge of the object to which it refers (whether that object exists independently of that knowledge or not). This object is grasped by the knowing subject when it is represented to him by the appropriate referring term as it is used in a proposition. It is language that conducts the knower to the object of knowledge. Realism and objectivism are the foundations of the referential theory of meaning.

Idealism is at best agnostic on the question of the independent existence of objects. But it denies that reference has anything to do with what gives meaning to a word. Hence, objectivism is denied, for idealism claims that when we know the meaning of a word we do not grasp a relation between the word and an object. The empiricist and idealist theories thus differ precisely in their understanding of representation. For empiricism, representation involves the making present of the object, if not in, then through the word. But idealism, insofar as it recognizes representation as a legitimate concept, claims that it is the mark of the absence of the object from propositional knowledge. The word doesn't so much stand *for* the object as it replaces it, pushes it out of the picture. Strictly speaking, however, idealism ought not to countenance representation as a semantic relation at all, since in its view the semantic value of a word belongs to the linguistic, not the language-independent realm.

When a speaker knows the meaning of a word, he does not therefore grasp a relation between a sign and a thing that exists independently of the sign. What he knows is the relation that holds between a sign and a concept, or as Saussure puts it, between a signifier and a signified. According to Saussure's analysis of language, semantic value (*'valeur'* – which is conceptual, not referential) is the product of a complex of relations holding between all the words in a given language-system (*'langue'*). A particular signified cannot be 'cut out' from the continuum of thought unless its dotted lines are fixed by a correlative signifier. But no one signifier all on its own will have a semantic value; rather, the identity of a given signifier's value is determined by the position it occupies as distinct from every other signifier in the system. The signified that corresponds to a signifier thus does not constitute a positive value. First, it is not a thought-content that subsists independently of the signifier, since its identity is determined by the signifier itself. Second, and this is a point that Derrida insists on, the signified cannot be grasped as such, for it is always giving way to other signifiers, much as a dictionary might lead us ever onward, from one definition to another (because the definition of one word consists of nothing but a string of different words). As Derrida says, the signified 'is always ready in the position of the signifier' (*Of Grammatology*, E p. 73; F p. 108). And just as there is no path leading outside the dictionary, so there is no going outside language and appealing to independent objects as the anchors of meaning.

That which gives content to our words is not so much subject-dependent as it is language-dependent. The idealist theory of meaning, so far from regarding Thought as causally efficacious in the non-discursive realm (cf Frege, 'The Thought' and 'Logik'), sees thought-content as the effect of a differentiation between signifiers.

Derrida, for instance, speaks of thought as 'the blank part of the text [*un blanc textuel*]', claiming that 'It is, in the play of the system, that very thing which never has weight' (*Of Grammatology*, E p. 93; F p. 142). We might say that, according to the idealist theory, the signified is caught within the system of signifiers in much the same way as a positron leaves a trace in a cloud chamber, and so is believed to be *there*, though it has no weight, is never seen.

Derrida's contribution to the idealist theory has been to fashion a more sophisticated version while criticizing its traditional and overt conceptualist tenets. Idealism as propounded by Saussure suggests that the signified is an unproblematic psychological content which, in a way never made clear, is established as a unit of meaning through being picked out by a signifier. This supposes that there is a mental fund or vein of thought-content that simply awaits individuation by an articulated system of marks. The trouble with this view is that it assumes the very thing it is trying to establish: that which would endow the sign with a determinate meaning. Derrida is especially critical of this way of looking at meaning since it strikes him as the founding thesis of logocentrism. He argues against the traditional conception of the signified as 'a meaning thinkable in principle within the full presence of an intuitive consciousness . . . outside of all signifiers' (*Of Grammatology*, E p. 73; F pp. 106–7). The alternative is not to abandon the signified in favour of a pure 'play of signifiers', but to return the signified from the realm of the transcendental to the immanent system of language. Derrida speaks with approval of Peirce's theory of a sign's meaning (though he misinterprets Peirce to his own advantage):

> Peirce goes very far in the direction that I have called the deconstruction of the transcendental signified, which, at one time or another, would place a reassuring end to the reference from sign to sign . . . he considers the indefiniteness of reference as the criterion that allows us to recognize that we are dealing with a system of signs. *What broaches the movement of signification is what makes its interruption impossible. The thing itself is a sign.* . . . The so-called 'thing-itself' is always already a *representamen*. . . . The *representamen* functions only by giving rise to an *interpretant* that itself becomes a sign and so on to infinity. The self-identity of the signified forever conceals and displaces itself.
> (*Of Grammatology*, E p. 49; F pp. 71–2)

Here we have in compressed form what Derrida claims to achieve by his deconstruction of the sign. It is not (or not simply), as some of his detractors have supposed, a destruction of the sign, whose 'unity of heterogeneities' Derrida conserves. Of course, neither is it a theory that tells us what a speaker knows when he knows the meaning of a sign. It is, however, a critique of the view of the signified as pure content. The sign's deconstruction is designed to rehabilitate the signified by fixing it within an inescapable domain of language (or text). Thus when Derrida says that the interruption of the movement of signification is impossible, he means that we can never, either by semantic theory or interpretative practice, bring to a halt the reference of one sign to another that constitutes signification. The signified, then would consist of a semantic deferral that is never-ending, since both routes out of the play of signification are closed to us. First, the thing itself is claimed to be a sign, so there is no arriving full-stop at a referent that would determinately settle for us the question of semantic value. Second, the signified is but one point in the chain linking one signifier to the next; so, at this end as well, there is no coming to rest at a concept that would fix the sign's content.

The odd thing about this 'deconstruction' of the sign is that its criticism is directed simultaneously at the empiricist *and* idealist theories of meaning. Derrida considers them to be equally logocentric, whether it be a question of the presence in the sign of meaning as referent or as concept. (This is perhaps most evident in the way Derrida casually interchanges the referential with the conceptual: he speaks of the signified as 'sense or thing, noeme or reality'. He might just as well have said 'referent or idea'.) Neverthless, I would insist that, in Derrida's hands, the significance of a sign, whether it be a text or a single signifier, is accounted for by a covert idealism, where semantic value is no longer the product of a direct relation of sign to concept, but of sign to sign. It is this version of the idealist theory of meaning that I call *metaphorical*.

If we use a simple model, then metaphor can be defined as the substitution of the literal signified in the sign-complex by a further, metaphorical signified. Consider, for example, an artless metaphor such as 'twilight' standing for old age. In a poem, the literal signified of 'twilight' will be the drawing to close of day, the end of light. But the metaphorical signified will be old age. Both the signifier *and* signified of the literal sign function as the signifier for the metaphorical content, old age. Whereas the artful metaphor dispenses with the intermediate signifier, 'old age', in order to take us directly from 'twilight' to its metaphorical signified, the artless metaphor makes explicit use of the intermediate signifier. If we say, somewhat prosaically, 'Old age is the twilight of life', we have made it rather obvious that one sign ('old age' and its meaning) is being substituted for the signified of another ('twilight'). By dint of its literal content, 'twilight' is associated with another sign altogether.

It is the prosaic metaphorical relation that I wish to apply to Derrida's tacit theory of meaning. Even in what is considered standard, or non-metaphorical, signification, the signified of one sign is thought to be usurped by another sign-complex, whose own signified is replaced by yet another sign-complex, and so on. In each case, the signifier of the succeeding sign serves as the signified of the preceding sign in the signifying chain. Thus the place of one sign's meaning is always being taken by another sign.[4]

Derrida evidently believes that the signified is therefore virtual only, a place holder in the sign-complex. I am not certain just what he thinks this does to the identity of the signified. As he said above, 'The self-identity of the signified forever conceals and displaces itself.' Perhaps he is granting that the signified has an identity but that it can never in fact be identified.

Whether I have his position exactly right or not, there is a difficulty here. In order for a signifier's meaning to be another sign-complex the signified must be identical with the replacing sign. It follows therefore that a given sign-complex is identifiable only if the signified it replaces is identifiable. But according to Derrida's theory, the signified is always indeterminate; thus the entire sign turns out to be of indeterminate identity. This wreaks havoc with any attempt to identify the sense of a word. And the problem is that the indeterminacy doesn't come at the level of the sign's significance as it is used in a particular text, but at the more fundamental level of its semantic value. I shall amplify on this distinction in the next section.

The metaphorical theory of meaning that I attribute to Derrida remains a form of idealism strictly speaking, for semantic value is produced entirely within the confines of the language, without reference to the world of things. (If we like, however, we can distinguish this form from the conceptualism Derrida attacks – the direct appeal to extra-linguistic thought-contents – by calling his idealism, not without a gnashing of teeth, significationism.)

When we know the meaning of a word, according to the metaphorical theory, we do not know its reference, nor its ability to affect the truth-conditions of declarative sentences. What we do know is something very much like what systematic semantics calls the *role* played by the word in th˄ language, i.e., the way it tends to behave in different grammat˄al contents. ('What', for instance, functions as a relative pronoun in some contexts, but as an interrogative pronoun in others.) In idealism the notion of a word's role might be called its signifying disposition: what chain of words the term is likely to appear in, how it supports the discursive work done by other words, or even how it might organize that work, as it might if it were one of the controlling concepts in a philosophical treatise. For example, in understanding a general term we know which particular terms tend to appear in its range within a text, and how that general term will entail the appearance of other general terms and the absence of yet others. (The notion of signifying disposition is closely, perhaps necessarily, linked to a word's use in *texts*. I shall return to this point below.)

Of course, the signifying disposition of a word will vary from one type of discourse to another, depending on whether the register is literary, scientific, philosophical, sociological, conversational, public, private, suasive, amorous, and so on. The tradition behind a particular mode of discourse will determine in part which words can and cannot appear, and how they will be interrelated. Thus historiographical discourse has built up a certain body of texts which sets an example of the discursive mode to be employed by succeeding historians. On the other hand, individual discursive practices are such that they are apt to introduce innovations into a particular mode, so that no type of discourse will remain absolutely static, either stylistically or thematically. (The conditions for the possibility of the introduction or deletion of certain terms and the signifying structures they entail will rest partly within the discursive paradigm itself and partly within the given socio-historical period during which the texts are formulated.) Finally, a particular type of discourse will be identifiable as such because of the presence of certain types of words along with their discursive organization. (A literary text, for instance, may make free use of the first person while a scientific text would normally be limited to the third.) Similarly, a word does not organize a set of particular terms *because* it is a general term; rather, the work qualifies as a general term because it tends to have such discursive powers.

The signifying-disposition theory presupposes that the words in a text are related to one another according to various discursive *structures* which govern their meaningful employment. These structures can in principle be discovered through a comparative analysis of texts belonging to the same discursive mode, as well as through a contrastive analysis of texts belonging to different modes.

The post-structuralist theory is at this point most like the neo-Fregean theory, for the notion of discursive structure can be linked to that of the *rules* comprising a language's logical grammar. These rules govern the word's contributions to the meanings of various propositions, while the overall logical grammar determines the presupposition and entailment relations that hold between different propositions. When we understand a general term, we know which inferences its use licences and which it rules out.

This way of looking at meaning has been cultivated in the semantics of formal logic and mathematics, where the language's regimentation makes the issues sharper than in the more complex and ambiguous natural languages. In a formal language, where particular terms are given precise semantic values, our understanding of sentential operators (the signs for conjunction, disjunction, negation, implication, and so forth) will be reflected by the body of accepted proofs in which those expressions play a part. Thus we want to know how a correct, or full, understanding of an expression's meaning may nevertheless fail to disclose to us every last one of the inferences licensed by the use of that expression. For imagine that a novel proof is constructed with the aid of a heretofore uncontroversial expression: we come to see, in that proof, an extension of the expression's semantic powers. But have we deepened our understanding of that expression, or have we instead changed its meaning, reinterpreted it? It is this sort of question that research into the notion of a language's structure, or logical grammar, helps us to answer.

So far, significationism and systematic semantics are in accord (though the former will be more sympathetic toward a constructivist than a realist semantics). But once we pass from structure and general terms down to the issue of particular terms significationism encounters difficulties. How will idealism, in default of a theory of reference, answer questions about the meanings of concrete terms such as the name 'water' or the predicate 'blue'? The only recourse would be to fix their meanings according to how they are organized by general terms. This requires that the meanings of the general terms already have been fixed. Yet this is precisely what the theory has not done: it has instead *assumed* meanings for particular terms and then looked to infer the meanings of general terms as they are used in a given text; and the structure of discursive relations thus uncovered may well be peculiar to that text. The general term 'truth', for example, will have in a text of Nietzsche's a signifying disposition quite different from the one it has in a text of Frege's. What is in question, however, is not the structural semantic relations that hold between words in a text, but what it is that lends semantic value to the word in the first place.

Significationism's answer is, if anything, less satisfying than classical Saussureanism. Saussure at least offered something as the content-supplier for the signifying forms – namely, concepts. And there is a suggestion in his writings that a referential treatment could be accommodated within his overall schema. But by rejecting conceptualism in favour of what I have called the metaphorical theory of meaning, Derrida (and other post-structuralists) have left language hanging, unanchored to anything that would lend determinate semantic values to its words. Once looked at closely, the metaphorical theory's picture of language as an immanent system of significations reveals serious flaws. What is at issue is not whether language's *structure* is self-contained, but whether language doesn't relate to the world in some way more direct than significationism is willing to admit.

If the signifying chain, whose last link is connected to the first, satisfactorily explains how words have determinate meanings, then the explanation ought to work for languages of decreasing complexity, even one so simple as to contain only a handful of terms, say, 'class', 'colour', 'blue', and 'brown'. According to how often the speakers of the language use their four words we might be able to conclude that 'class' was the most general of the terms, 'colour' was nested within it, and 'blue' and 'brown' within 'colour'. But, barring recourse to the notion of reference, how should we make sense of that hierarchy? We can imagine discovering a dictionary for the language, whose definitions would tell us how the words are related: blue and brown are types of colour, colour is a type of class. For all that, we remain stuck in the dictionary until we can obtain another kind of definition altogether – an ostensive one that will demonstrate to us what falls under the extensions of 'blue' and 'brown'. Without a referential theory (or some other theory that will show us that words are related to the world as we speak of it) we are given no semantic ingress to the language. The significationist theory of linguistic structure is not vitiated, but it can no longer pretend to be an adequate semantic theory. It's as though we were given form without content.

The problem with the significationism that underlies Derrida's lectural approach is not one about its holistic structure. In this respect the theory has strong affinities with a strand of empiricist semantics, Quine's linguistic holism. The problem lies where the significationist picture differs from Quine: at the first level of a language's semantic content.

According to Quine, the meaning of a word is fixed by its reference, but the identity of the referent cannot be determined except relative to a language. For suppose there is a referring expression, 'gavagai'. In order for the word to have a semantic value for us we must be able to identify its referent as distinct from the referents of other words: we must have a criterion of identity. If we lack such criteria, the objects in question will not, in and of themselves, lose their distinctiveness; but they will lose their semantic value for the speaker, since he will be unable to distinguish one from another. Thus Quine's famous dictum, 'No entity without identity'. Yet how shall we fix the identity of the referent of 'gavagai'? As foreign speakers we could note the contexts for the native's use of the word until we had established to our satisfaction the criteria that must obtain for its use to be warranted. But the specification of those criteria will be couched in our language, something like 'fleet, small, furry animal with long ears'. Thus we will have come up with a tentative interpretation of the foreign word in our own language, translating 'gavagai' as 'rabbit'. Still, we will have no guarantee that the referents of the two words are precisely the same. Quine maintains there is no question here of fact, since there is no absolute, language-independent means of specifying the thing's criterion of identity; as he puts it, 'reference is non-sense except relative to a system of co-ordinates' ('Ontological Relativity', p. 48).

Because there is no such thing as language-independent meaning, we have nothing against which to judge the correctness of empirically equivalent translations. There is no deciding whether 'X' really ought to be rendered as 'A' or as 'B'. And even if we eschew meanings in favour of referents, the indeterminacy persists. (We might regard the meaning of an expression as consisting in its use to refer to a particular object.) Quine thwarts fixing the exact referent as well, for he holds that reference is inscrutable: at bottom we cannot tell whether 'gavagai' refers to rabbits, rabbit-stages, or collections of rabbit-parts.

The claim for the inscrutability of reference depends on Quine's argument that theories in general are underdetermined by evidence. We haven't any method for discovering exactly what it is the foreign speaker is referring to (what he means to refer to) in using 'gavagai'; we can only represent his reference in our language. Moreover, some other interpretation might fit equally well with the evidence. So we are left with translations instead of meanings or references. When we give the meaning of a word in language L' we can appeal only to our own language L. Yet if the references of words in L' are given in terms of L, then the references of L itself must likewise be language-relative (from the point of view of L'-speakers). Hence the meaning of a word is determinate only to the extent that it is part of an overall translation for the language.

This does not mean that the theory of meaning, insofar as it is a theory of translation, forgoes reference entirely. Just because the reference of a foreign word is ultimately inscrutable, it doesn't mean that the words of the language do not refer. The attack is not so much on reference as a semantic relation as on our certainty that we can determine just what the reference is. Indeed, a successful theory of translation needn't spell out how reference (or ostension, or demonstration) actually works; it needn't even decide what the 'true' referent is in a given case. But it does rely on the referential relation holding in general between objects and the words of the language. Reference, as far as a theory of translation goes, is a relation that happens to hold. *That* it holds is sufficient for the translator; *why* it holds does not worry him.

Looking at language in this way does comport to some extent with Derrida's views. First, the question of an absolute, 'correct' meaning is undecidable. Second, semantics turns out to be a task of interpretation, though not, it is true, of texts, but of entire languages. For example, Donald Davidson's truth-conditional semantics is based on Quine's idea of radical translation. Davidson suggests that by looking at the principle by which we interpret one language's propositions in terms of another's (i.e., the specification of the truth-conditions of a proposition in L' by means of a proposition in L), we get a deep insight into the nature of linguistic meaning. Insofar as Davidson's programme makes truth-conditions its central concept, it, like Quine's, remains a referential, and hence empiricist, semantics. Whereas for empiricism understanding a word consists in knowing a relation that holds between the discursive and non-discursive realms, for Derridean idealism understanding a word consists in knowing a relation that holds entirely within the discursive realm.

The sharpest contrast between the two theories can be brought out by comparing Quine's view of the holistic structure of language with Derrida's. According to Quine (in *Word and Object*), the periphery of language is made up of a corpus of observation-sentences expressing what we know about the world through direct experience and testing. Language finds its edge when it runs up against non-discursive states of affairs. As we work our way toward the centre our sentences become less observational and more theoretical, the connections between them being the inferential steps we take from the raw data to sophisticated hypotheses. At the very centre of the structure articulated by all these inferences lie the most hypothetical of our propositions, the ones from which we are most likely to withdraw belief under pressure. The direction of epistemological influence in this model always runs inward: we revise the tentative hypotheses at the centre (and sometimes even the more firmly believed propositions nearer the edge) under the impress of our changing observations of the world. And on occasion, radically new empirical discoveries will necessitate wholesale revision of the structure of our beliefs. The court of final appeal lies at the periphery, where our language touches on the world and is given meaning.

For Derrida language is a structure that is self-contained, with no identifiable periphery. Moreover, the direction of influence is seen to run the other way, since that which confers meaning on our sentences lies at the centre. But he criticizes the idea that the centre is the location of an original meaning or signified that anchors all other significations. In fact, Derrida argues that the centre is not locatable, that when we came to recognize the principle of linguistic structure in and for itself we discovered that there could be no fixed and identifiable origin of meaning. He speaks of 'a system in which the central signified, the original and transcendental signified, is never absolutely present outside a system of differences', and goes on to say that 'The absence of [such a] signified extends to infinity the domain and play of signification' ('Structure, Sign and Play', E p. 280; F p. 411). This play is never brought to a halt, for the *res* is always absent from the word. Knowledge of meaning therefore would not involve empirical knowledge.

Interpretation and intention

The charge I have levelled against the idealist semantic theory found in post-structuralism is that it fails to give us any clues as to why our words are meaningful, either in terms of a referential relation holding between sign and thing or in terms of what a speaker must know if he is to understand the language. The other alternative, the simple conceptualist explanation, remains circular so long as we are not told what it is to have a concept in terms other than knowing the meaning of a word. In and of itself this failing cannot be imputed to Derrida, since he nowhere proposes a theory of meaning for natural language. But he can be taxed with basing his lecturalism upon a faulty semantic theory – insofar as he embraces significationism as I have outlined it. A theory addressed to the meanings of words as they function in texts is at best incomplete without an account of the meanings those words carry into the text, for the textual work a word does must derive from a standard meaning that it bears in the language at large, outside of any one text. An interpretation of the latter sort must assign the word a determinate meaning, so that it can then be used to such-and-such an effect within, or, if we like, *by* the text. I shall call this the first level of interpretation, and its assignments of first-order meanings assign-ments of a word's sense.

When a radical translator seeks to interpret a foreign language, using only the speakers' behaviour (in a context) as data, he is trying to assign each word a determinate (language-relative) sense. The interpretation he gives will be a hypothesis designed to cover all the linguistic behaviour observed up to that point. In this respect the theory of meaning is an empirical one: presented with a collection of data, the theorist constructs a working hypothesis, revising it accord-ingly as new data contradict or confirm it. Testing the hypothesis will consist in presenting the native speakers with certain propositions in various context and seeing whether they assent to them or not. (This is an important point, one to which I shall return below.) The goal is to assign a sense to every word, thereby providing an exhaustive interpretation of the language, allegedly based only on what is empirically verifiable (i.e., without recourse to any semantic concepts in the explanans).

Even if, along with Quine, we regard the translation as indeterminate, and admit that some other, conflicting account might just as plausibly interpret the speakers' linguistic behaviour, the senses we assign to the words are themselves determinate relative to our frame of translation (since the choice of individual translations is dictated by the overall schema). The interpretation of a language is seen to involve the assignment of first-order meanings only. It is not yet a question of trying to find out what those words, endowed with determinate senses, are themselves used to say. This involves a second-order meaning, and it is at this level that the interpretation of texts operates.

By second-level interpretation I mean any assignment of meaning that assumes a semantic value for the words (or other signs) under consideration. The 'data' have already been subjected to one interpretation. It is on the basis of an assignment of senses to the words that any second-level interpretation can occur. At this level, interpretation is an answer to the question, what are these words, with such-and-such meanings, being used to do? Or: what move in the language-game is being made by means of these words? Do they serve to make an assertion, pose a question, deliver a warning, knock down an argument, persuade us to act in a certain way, tell a tale, a joke, or a lie? We are asking not what the sense of these words is, but what they mean, what they wish to say.

It will be noticed that the graduation from first to second-order meaning imports a new element into the semantic realm: intention. As soon as we ask what the words mean, in the sense of wish to say, we are asking what is meant by them, what they are intended to do. This is standardly the province of speech-act theory, in which utterances (or texts) are assessed as types of action undertaken by a linguistic agent, i.e., as involving reference to the agent's beliefs and desires as they would figure in a specification of the motivations or goals of that action. (Not everything an agent does is an action. An action must have at least one intentional description, which is to say that it must be explainable in terms of the agent's desires and beliefs: the *cause* of the action is the agent's *reason* for acting.)

The introduction of an intentional element when talking about second-order meaning should not be surprising. Whether we look at it from the point of view of the actor or the interpreter there must be some linguistic agent who grasps the first-order sense of the words. On the one hand, if a writer is using the words to make a move in the language-game, he must grasp their senses under some scheme of interpretation. On the other hand, if a reader is to understand something by those words, he must assume not only that the individual words have senses, but that someone inscribed them in this particular order because he intended to say something with them. Of course it is always possible that the reader, though he recognizes the various words, will be able to make nothing of them at the second level. If so, he may think that the writer intended to produce a non-sensical text. Notice, however, that even at this juncture the reader is inclined to attribute an intentional description to the collection of words, since without some such description the 'writing' ceases to function as a text. In that case, instead of non-sense, the reader would regard the words (though individually sensical) as making *no* sense whatsoever. They might be thought to have tumbled accidentally onto the page.

Second-order meaning, then, necessarily involves an understanding of the language's words as they are deployed in the utterance (whether spoken or written) in order to effect a linguistic act. First-order meaning, or sense, involves no such understanding. The words of a language may all have determinate senses without therefore being used for or interpreted as saying something. (I do not say: 'without having ever been used'!) No linguistic agent need be involved for a word-type or one of its tokens to have a sense. It has that sense in virtue of belonging to a language, not in virtue of its use on a particular occasion. English words on an eye-chart, for example, each have a determinate sense according to a first-level interpretation for the language; but they do not mean or wish to say anything as they are displayed on the chart. (In this case the words are being used for something other than a language-game.)

The grasp of second-order meaning presupposes a grasp of the words' senses. The difference between the two sorts of meaning can be likened to that between the sense and force of a sentence as uttered and the point of making the utterance. The same group of words – 'is', 'raining', 'it' – can be uttered with different forces, though the individual words do not alter their senses. 'It is raining.' is said with assertoric force, while 'Is it raining?' is uttered with interrogative force. Our understanding of the forces will depend in part on our understanding of the words' senses.

(Conversely, I believe it can be argued that the grasp of a word's sense requires a grasp of, minimally, what it is to assert something. This is so to the extent that our understanding of a word depends on knowing how it is used in sentences with determinate truth-values. Since only sentences that are asserted can admit of truth-conditions, there can be no purchase on sense until we see what assertion involves. In this respect force may be regarded as conceptually prior to sense.)

The point of saying something refers to what it is we mean to effect by the utterance, such as scolding, promising, lying, joking, reporting, and so forth. Like force, the point of an utterance may change though the sense does not. But the force itself may also remain the same. For example, two utterances of 'It is raining.', indistinguishable in terms of their sense and force, may have quite different points, for the first may be the truth while the second is a lie (not just a false report). The point of the latter is to mislead the audience, while the point of the former is to inform them correctly.

Taking account of the point of an utterance is to read an intention into the words, for it imputes a particular goal to the utterer. When we ask what is meant by the expression on an occasion of use, we are not asking after its literal sense. We take for granted the first-order meaning of 'Will you stay another night?': we know its sense and its force. What we want to know is its second-order meaning, whether it is a question or an invitation. The interpretation we bring to bear upon the utterance thus recalls Montaigne's suggestion that we interpret interpretations. This is precisely what Derrida's project of reading a text is about: an attempt to find in it a second-order meaning. At this level there will naturally be more divergence in interpretations. We might all agree on the senses of the constituent words, but produce entirely different readings. And at key points there will even be arguments over just what a word means in a given context. In some cases, like the central philosophical concepts of a text, a grasp of the sense of the word will be counted as incomplete without a grasp of its second-order meaning – the work it does within the discourse. (A Fregean Thought is quite different from a thought as we normally understand the concept.)

What lecturalism lacks is a first-order theory of meaning, one that would fix the senses of a language's expressions. Its programme of reading is aimed instead at second-order meaning, at which level, so the argument goes, the text achieves autonomy, opening itself up to an interpretation that need not account for the original intention of the author. But I would have thought that the real autonomy is to be found at the first level, where the meanings of the expressions are determined by that which transcends individual intentions, namely, the grammatical rules and assignments of sense fixed by the language itself, and not by any one reader. Derrida is surely right in pointing out that the question of second-order meaning is ultimately undecidable. Often there are utterances whose point cannot be determined with any certainty unless we ask the author to make his intention explicit, and appeals of this sort cannot be made to absent or dead authors. Moreover, even when the utterer is available we haven't any guarantee that his explanation will be in principle more plausible than ours. Whether written or spoken, the text does have a certain life of its own.

But now I want to ask, if, as Derrida claims, writing is entirely cut off from the intentions of the author, in what respect does it still warrant the description 'writing'? How can a string of words constitute a text if they cannot be read as having an intentional description? In reading, we may not be able to establish the author's original intention; but if that print (or script) is denuded of all intentional character, it ceases to be writing, for writing, perhaps more than anything, is an intentional activity. Since a text never functions as a text unless it can be read (or at least be seen as readable), whether by the author or another reader, I am stressing the interpretative, not the productive side of the issue. It is how the interpreter reads the object, as the product of an intentional action (or, alternatively, as the product of simple physical motions) that is crucial to his interpretation.

This is equally true for the radical translator, who needs to be armed at least with the intentional notions of assent and dissent if he is to discover how (even whether) the creatures under scrutiny are speaking a language. The task of interpreting another human natural language (such as Gavagaiese) does not throw into sharp enough relief just how much tacit understanding of the way language works the translator must possess before he can even begin to guess at truth-conditions. (Quine's argument for the practical inscrutability of reference is plausible only if Gavagai-speakers have a form of life significantly different from our own – e.g., with respect to their perceptual capacities.)

If he were confronted with the behaviour of an alien race, the decision whether they were speaking a language would in part hinge on whether their utterances were counted as intentional or not. Were the translator unable to characterize the 'utterances' in terms of the 'speaker's' beliefs and desires, there would be good reason to doubt the creature was *speaking* a language as we conceive of the activity. It might be biologically programmed to produce a variety of complex signals in response to changes in its environment. But so far as the translator regards these 'utterances' as physical reactions rather than as actions, he has no basis for counting the data as linguistic behaviour. A thermometer reacts to its environment in a rule-governed, informative way, but it does not speak a language.

The problem of the text's intentional origin is even more acute in the case of writing. We treat the written text as sensical because we take its marks to be indications of someone having said, i.e., written, something. But imagine the discovery of a tablet inscribed with a fairly regular pattern of marks that do not belong to any known language. Before the radical translator attempts to interpret the marks, that is, before he can treat the tablet as a text, he must decide whether they are intentional inscriptions or purely accidental, a chance product of natural forces. A text, insofar as it is an artifact written by someone, must admit of an intentional description. The recovery of that person's *particular* intentions, in terms of the second-order meaning he had in mind, is a secondary (though equally important) question.

My claim is that the notion of intention is indispensable if the lecturalist reader's and the radical translator's programmes of interpretation are to get off the ground. For the former because no sense can be made of writing except as the mark of an intentional activity; for the latter because a speaker's assent, even if its manifestation is behaviourally characterized, is identified as such according to an intentional description (based on the translator's native knowledge of what it is to assent to a proposition in his own language). I am not thereby claiming that actions such as assent and writing must be characterized in intentional vocabulary. If a satisfactory reduction of the intentional to the physical could be produced (though I don't believe one could) then intentions as entities could be avoided, in favour of the brain states that would identify them. But the explanatory role of intentions in semantic theory must be taken by something;

they cannot simply be dismissed, or ignored, as Derrida wishes to do.

I have not said *how* intentions are to be fitted in to a formal account of first- and second-order meaning; I have only tried to show that they must be fitted in if the semantic theory is to be successful. I should also make it clear that any satisfying theory must address the way in which first-order semantic values generally depend on an intentional base, even though the semantic relation itself need have no intentional aspect. First, because before the sense of an expression can be determined it is necessary to settle the question of whether the production of certain sounds or marks is to be counted as speaking a language. This cannot be decided except (minimally) by reference to the concept of assertoric force, for an informant's assent to a proposition is the exemplar of his asserting (and thus believing) something to be true. Our understanding of assent is based on our understanding of what it is to believe something and to desire to communicate that belief.

The second reason why a theory of first-order meaning depends on our grasp of the intentional has to do with the nature of reference. Reference as a relation is to some extent a concoction of semantic theory: the relation is defined as holding between the names of the language and their so-called bearers – for whatever reason. How or why the relation holds isn't what determines the individual expression's denotational value. Nevertheless, it is the how-and-why that makes the name-bearer relation possible. Whereas, say, Davidson's method does aim for interpretations, it doesn't bring to light the foundation of the semantic relation he assumes to be holding. To the extent that meaning is based on reference, as the empiricists claim (or at least assume), our understanding of it must remain imperfect as long as our understanding of reference itself is faulty. In this respect, a theory of translation will be insufficient as a theory of meaning because it doesn't make clear that the *relation* of reference depends on an *act* of reference. (Here I am arguing not about particular cases in the body of a linguistic practice, but about the background of a semantic relation.) Referring is something the speaker does. As much as the sentence's having a truth-value depends on its being uttered with a particular force, so the word cannot have a reference unless some speaker (sometime) intended it to refer. It is just this intentional basis of reference that a first-order interpretation glosses over, though its ultimate success is linked directly to an understanding of that basis. Even if we accept the minimal requirement of radical translation, that the theory need spell out only that knowledge which the translator must possess in order to arrive at an understanding of the foreign language, something will have to be said about his (pre-reflective) grasp of the connection between intention and reference, for without any such grasp the interpretation would never get started. In one respect, then, it can be said that a theory of intention must underlie a theory of reference (and sense). The intentional does not always inhere in the referential relation, but it does provide the ground of possibility for that relation.

The distinction I have drawn between first- and second-order meaning is not confined to natural language. It holds wherever the object of interpretation is a sign endowed with some sort of sense. The interpretation of non-linguistic actions seeks to determine the second-order meaning of behaviour which itself has already been semantically characterized. The behaviour will qualify as an action, such as throwing a ball or bowing in obeisance, only if it admits of a description involving reference to the agent's beliefs and desires. This description needn't be supplied by the agent himself, nor even couched in his own language; the behaviour might instead be lent a sense by a radical translator.

The salient difference in the case of non-linguistic action is that the identification of the bit of behaviour to be interpreted already involves an intentional description. Just as we discriminate the lexical unit (the individual aural or graphic signifier) in linguistic interpretation, so we must decide whether a bodily movement is an action or not (for example, an involuntary motion). To use Davidson's term, the action is 'primitive' under a given description, one that simply identifies the bodily movement. Once we have identified the behavioural bit, say, moving the finger, we can proceed to give it a first-level interpretation *qua* action, say, pointing. The intentional aspect that allows us to characterize the movement as an act of pointing is what distinguishes the object of the first-level interpretation of non-linguistic behaviour from the word as the object of first-level linguistic interpretation. Whereas both the word and the behavioural bit must fall under some intentional description in order to qualify as objects of interpretation, the sense of the word does not, from case to case, depend on the agent's intention in using it. However, the first-order meaning of the primitive action depends directly on the agent's intention (or the intention imputed to him). The extension of a finger is a movement, but it is not an action unless it is intentional.

The further attempt to assess the significance of that behaviour, *characterized as a particular action*, amounts to a second-level interpretation. The character of a primitive action may change according to its context and consequences. The repeated curling of a finger in one context might be a signal to come; but in another context the same action might involve the pulling of a trigger, and hence the shooting of a gun. Depending on the consequences of the act, the shooting might count as target practice or as killing. Moreover, the cause of the action will distinguish an inadvertent killing from an act of murder, depending on whether the agent desired to kill the victim and believed that he could do so by shooting the gun.

First-level interpretation identifies a movement as a primitive action; second-level interpretation identifies an action as an act within a concrete physical and social context. At one level we determine the sense of a movement – an action; at the other level we determine the meaning of the action – an act. (Thus we speak of pulling a trigger or pointing a finger as actions, but of their consequences as acts – an act of murder, an act of betrayal. Uttering is an action too, but it can also be a speech act.)

Differentiating a second-level of interpretation from the first enables us to make sense of the popular distinction between the natural and the human sciences. The former treat of data that call for a first-level interpretation only (hence physics, chemistry, biology). The latter treat of data that call for at least a second-level interpretation. The human agent has already intervened in the object of analysis, whose intentional character helps us to identify it as a text, inscribed in speech, writing, or action (hence anthropology, history, psychoanalysis).

It is interesting that empiricism has been identified with methodology in the natural sciences, while post-structuralism has been linked with the human sciences. I have suggested that the idealist theory of meaning which supports post-structuralism tends to militate against an understanding of the human subject. This is especially true of Derridean lecturalism, where the agent, along with the intentional, is pushed right out of the picture of textual meaning. Human science begins to look remarkably anti-humanist.

To pull the intentional back into the frame complicates the picture, but it also makes it truer to life. Figuring out how intentions are related to sense is of a piece with understanding how the subjective is related to the objective, the mind to the body, or the author to the text. While it may be expedient, in the face of dauntingly complex equations, to factor out the troublesome term, the attempt to eliminate the category of the intentional from semantic theory can hardly be deemed a promising start toward a solution.[5]

4

Critical Theory: Between Ideology and Philosophy

Michael Rosen

English speaking readers interested in the Critical Theory of the Frankfurt School have been well served in recent years. Almost all the school's major works have now been translated and several scholarly studies have appeared. Two questions have nevertheless been somewhat under-represented – their status as philosophers and the intellectual consistency of the school. The reasons are, I believe, connected.[1]

It is understandable that the purely philosophical aspect of Critical Theory should have received disproportionately little attention in Britain and America. Although the leading members of the school were trained and continued to regard themselves as philosophers, their writings first attracted attention abroad from sociologists, literary theorists and dissident Marxists, rather than academic philosophers. Working as they did within boundaries set by Kant, Hegel and Marx there hardly appeared to be a bridge of common concern connecting their problems to the anti-metaphysical Anglo-Saxon philosophical scene of Russell, Wittgenstein and Carnap.

Theodor Adorno's stay as an exile in Oxford in the thirties illustrates the gulf between the two worlds. Adorno complains in a letter that he can find no colleagues in the Oxford of Ayer, Ryle, Austin and Berlin sophisticated enough to appreciate his work: 'to make my philosophical affairs comprehensible to the English is an impossibility, and I must reduce my work to a somewhat childish level to continue to be understood'. Ayer, on the other hand, hardly regarded Adorno as a serious philosopher. He recalls him in his autobiography as 'a comic figure with his dandified manner and appearance'. The young philosophers of Oxford were, Ayer says, 'more amused than impressed' by Adorno's expressed interest in the philosophy of music. Clearly, neither was prepared to make concessions in order to appreciate the other.

I believe that this neglect of the philosophical dimension of Critical Theory has led to the second omission: a lack of satisfactory answers to the question of the school's intellectual coherence. Studies have concentrated on individual authors, and it is significant that the distinguished exception – Martin Jay's *The Dialectical Imagination* – breaks off at just the time after the war when the common identity of the school started to be seriously challenged. But this leaves behind a large question: was the school's undeniable break-up simply the passing of an episode in 'Weimar culture'?; or was it, at least in part, the result of difficulties and indeterminacies implicit in the original enterprise?

The answer that I shall suggest is essentially this: the school's initial programme was, indeed, equivocal. Thus subsequent developments are best understood as a series of competing attempts to make that programme coherent and philosophically acceptable by resolving its original ambiguities.

Kant against Marx: Marx against Kant

To understand the perspective from which the programme of Critical Theory was developed it is helpful to refer back from the twentieth century to an earlier 'critical philosophy': that of Kant. As Kant described it, the task of philosophy was to set up a 'court-house of reason'. The legal metaphor carries important implications for the way in which the task of philosophy is conceived. The metaphor suggests, first, that philosophy is a *normative* discipline. Like a court it has to adjudicate disputes brought before it. Those disputes, it is important to note, are not solely the product of philosophical speculation, but arise in the course of the everyday operation of the human mind, as part of its 'natural dialectic'. Philosophers, then, are not parasites on the intellectual community. Although they can provide no substantive knowledge (and are pernicious impostors if they claim to) their function is indispensable in setting standards and establishing boundaries.

The court-house metaphor carries a concomitant implication for the manner in which philosophical issues are to be resolved. They are neither to be decided *dogmatically* – in response to some authority whose legitimacy consists solely in its established power – nor *sceptically* bypassed. Within the court's domain philosophers are engaged in a kind of *philosophical jurisprudence*, making use only of what it is open to reason to determine. This is why Kant, his thinking interwoven as ever with the political vision of the Enlightenment, compares philosophy's role in bringing peace to the 'battlefield of metaphysics' with the political order of the *Rechtsstaat*, established with the foundation of civil society.

But what is the extent of reason's competence? To answer this Kant employs another, yet more famous, metaphor: philosophy is to carry out a *Copernican revolution*. Philosophical disputes would be incapable of resolution were the questions involved questions about the ultimate structure of a reality independent of the human mind. But they are not. They concern a reality which has been (in some sense) *produced*, whose features have been constituted by the activity of a non-empirical agency, the *transcendental subject*. What we have made (or 'constituted') we can know – not because transcendental activity is directly an object of our conscious perception but because its effects can be determined by a process of philosophical argument.

Kant's normative conception of philosophy forms a deliberate contrast to that of his predecessor, Locke. For, although Locke's *Essay* had also aimed to draw boundaries (it aspired, Locke wrote, to 'inquire into the original, certainty and extent of human knowledge') the method which it used was psychological and descriptive: Kant refers to it as a 'physiology of the mind'. Locke's psychological programme remained exceptionally influential, especially among the thinkers of the French Enlightenment, where it was developed into the 'philosophy of common sense'. At the end of the eighteenth century the school of social thinkers led by Destutt de Tracy actually chose a new name to differentiate their study of the origins and determinants of ideas from normative conceptions of philosophy. They called their discipline *idéologie*. Yet from Germany the school's identity seemed clear: *idéologie*, says Hegel, is 'pure Lockeanism'.

Ironically, by the time that Karl Marx came to elaborate his own programme for the positive understanding of ideas in society in the *German Ideology* the name had come to signify something different, philosophy which operated in abstraction from social reality; and the arch-ideologist was none other than Kant himself: the 'whitewashing spokesman' of the German petit-bourgeoisie, Marx calls him with characteristic good temper.

The result is that, whereas Marx took himself to be eliminating philosophy in favour of social science, from the Kantian point of view he appeared to be taking Locke's side in a specifically philosophical dispute. Critical Theory in the twentieth century moves in this tension between Kant and Marx. It attempts to recognize the rootedness of ideas in history and society without supporting Locke against Kant and so abandoning philosophy's claim to normative rationality. Marxism had only abolished philosophy in various ways; Critical Theory set out to interpret it. Its solution involved the reinterpretation of the Kantian concept of the *transcendental subject*: no longer a nodal point below the surface of consciousness its true identity was to be shown to be social and historical.

Traditional and Critical Theory

This claim about the transcendental subject plays a fundamental role in Max Horkheimer's 'Traditional and Critical Theory'. This essay, written in 1937, forms a natural starting point for discussion, for it was commonly acknowledged by the Frankfurt School's members as the classic statement of their programme. As we shall see, it was not the programme of the essay itself but how that programme could be specified and realized that was to divide later writings.

'Traditional and Critical Theory' starts by explaining the opposition announced by its title. What traditional theorists have in common, according to Horkheimer, is that they take theory to be incorporated in its purest form in the propositions of natural science. Thus philosophers in other respects so widely separated as Descartes, Mill and Husserl are all classed as traditional theorists. In the name of Critical Theory Horkheimer denies that the natural sciences represent such a cognitive ideal. Such an ideal of theory is not universal but the product of a specific historical situation: 'The traditional idea of theory is based on scientific activity as carried on within the division of labour at a particular stage in the latter's development' ('Traditional and Critical Theory', E p. 212; G p. 146).[2]

In universalizing this activity into a timeless norm the traditional conception of theory embodies a preconception of knowledge as the essentially passive reflection by a thinking subject of a neutral, mind-independent reality: 'The whole perceptible world . . . is seen by the perceiver as a sum-total of facts; it is there and must be accepted'. ('Traditional and Critical Theory', E p. 212; G p. 148).

Horkheimer, however, counters this picture with a thoroughly Kantian claim: reality as we know it is *constituted*. If the world is, as Wittgenstein once said, a world 'of facts not of things', then to treat those facts as neutral and ontologically independent is simply to reassimilate them to things and so to miss what is, in Horkheimer's view, paramount: facts embody human activity: 'The perceived fact is . . . codetermined by human ideas and concepts, even before its conscious theoretical elaboration by the knowing individual' (Traditional and Critical Theory', E p. 214; G p. 149). Now, how this 'codetermination' or 'constitution' takes place is, of course, the crucial point. It results, Horkheimer says, from the activity of society which is (in contrast to the passive individuals who comprise it) essentially an active subject. But in what way is society's 'activity' to be conceived? Indeed, given that, as individuals, the standpoint of society as an active whole is not open to us, what is to prove that the activity is taking place at all?

Implicitly, as I shall show, Horkheimer deals with four distinct sorts of constituting social activity in the course of the essay. Explicitly, however, he makes only one fundamental distinction: between constituting activity which is *subjective* and that which is *objective*: 'The facts which our senses present to us are socially preformed in two ways: through the historical character of the object perceived and through the historical character of the perceiving organ'. (Traditional and Critical Theory', E p. 213; G p. 149).

In asserting that facts are preformed because of the 'historical character' of the perceiving organ Horkheimer is clearly committing himself to an *instrumentalist* epistemology. (The name, although standard for views which connect the possession of concepts to human beings' activity, is potentially misleading, since it suggests that this activity always has an instrumental – i.e. means-end – character. Critical Theory vigorously disputes this claim.) To use Karl Popper's vivid metaphor, Horkheimer opts for a 'searchlight' rather than a 'bucket' theory of perception. The subject's encounter with reality is always informed by a prior conceptual framework; all perception is interpretation: 'The individual, however, receives sensible reality . . . into his world of ordered concepts. The latter . . . have developed along with the life process of society' ('Traditional and Critical Theory', E p. 215, G p. 151).

In accepting this, Horkheimer's way is opened for an important claim: if the framework of our concepts has been determined by the historical life process of society then there exists, perhaps, a form of activity whose particular role it is to change and develop those concepts and this, of course, is Critical Theory.

I turn now to the determination of the *object* (by which one means, properly speaking, *objective facts*) by society. What is involved in this conception is less easily established. According to Horkheimer the role of social action in the determination of the object increases with a society's capacity to affect and control the environment: 'The sensible world which a member of industrial society sees about him every day bears the mark of deliberate work.' ('Traditional and Critical Theory', E p. 214; G p. 150).

Yet this claim contains a significant ambiguity. The fact of human beings' effect upon their environment is beyond dispute: its philosophical significance is arguable, however. Specifically, does the undeniable fact that human beings transform their environment amount to the idea that facts are *constituted* by society in a way corresponding to that in which German Idealism had claimed they were constituted by the transcendental subject? I think that the idea that the two are equivalent derives from a failure to distinguish two different ways in which human activity might be said to *determine* an object. In the first case human activity determines an object when a reference to human actions features as part of the material, causal history of a phenomenon. In this sense the effects of human labour are an indisputable part of our world. An example would be the way in which climatologists take into consideration the effects of human habitation – the clearing of jungle, the pollution of cities – in order to determine future developments. It is clear that such actions are not dealt with *as actions* in the science. The phenomena which incorporate them can (indeed *must*) be reidentified by the scientist in purely physical terms – as a decrease in oxygen, increase in atmospheric sulphur, or whatever – in order to figure in the explanation; from the scientific standpoint it is extrinsic that they are at the same time purposeful human actions.

In contrast to this there is a second class of cases where the reference to human activity may be said to play a truly *constitutive* role in determining an object; this is where reference to the purposes of human agents is necessary to establish the very identity of the object in question. We could not establish that a bicycle was a *bicycle* or a house a *house* except with reference to the purposes embodied in its construction and use. Even the purely physical criteria which the object must meet in order to be a bicycle or a house derive from these purposes; a house is an enclosed space *because* it is intended to provide shelter for human beings, for example.

So far, then, I have distinguished three levels of constituting activity: (1) An *epistemological* level (corresponding to Horkheimer's *subjective* determination) on which the concepts are determined by means of which we perceive the world. (2) A *material* level on which human actions have concrete causal effects upon objects. (3) An *ontological* level on which reference to human purposes and intentions plays an indispensable role in establishing the identity of the object in question. To these must be added a fourth kind of constituting social activity which plays an important role in Horkeimer's essay, although it does not fit neatly into his official division between the 'subjective' and the 'objective' determination of facts. This is: (4) The constituting activity of the *will*.

Evidently the activity of the will does not play a role in determining facts in general but only those which are properly seen as (or as embodying) actions. Horkheimer, however, does not state this limitation, leaving open the suspicion that he does not make it; perhaps because he assumes that all facts are, indeed, actions. The suspicion would appear harsh were it not that just this thesis is fundamental to German Idealism. Facts are actions for Idealism, not because all facts incorporate individuals' empirical wills, but because all phenomena incorporate the transcendental, self-realizing activity of *Geist*.

According to Horkheimer, actions are truly intelligible only to the extent that the will which is realized in them is transparent to itself. The will is transparent insofar as it is rational and collective. Thus social action within the capitalist economic order is only imperfectly comprehensible; for capitalism presents itself to the awareness of individuals in the guise of an impersonal mechanism. Its role as the realization of a collective will is at the same time concealed behind the deceptive appearance of a 'second nature':

> [Men] experience the fact that society is comparable to non-human natural processes, to pure mechanisms, because cultural forms which are supported by war and oppression are not the creations of a unified, self-conscious will. . . . Reason cannot

become transparent to itself as long as men act as members of an organism which lacks reason.

('Traditional and Critical Theory', E pp. 218–19, G pp. 156–7)

Because not all facts can be assumed to be actions it is particularly important to distinguish this fourth level of constituting activity, by which actions are partial realizations of social will, from the third, ontological level, in which reference is made to human purposes in order to identify objects. If the two levels are conflated, every case in which we must refer to intentions in order to identify an object must be seen as incorporating, as intrinsic to that identification, an aspiration towards the self-realization of a collective subject. This is a very strong claim indeed: for surely we can identify a house as a *house* without needing to anticipate the architecture of some future emancipated society. The assumption that the true identity of an object can only be established by viewing it *sub specie emancipationis* implies a dependence of meaning on history with its ancestry in Hegel's teleology of *Geist* – by no means a trivial assumption.

The four levels of constitution are, then, logically distinct, and if they do, indeed, mutually entail one another then this requires a philosophical demonstration which Horkheimer does not provide. Yet he moves between all four levels in his conception of Critical Theory.

Critical Theory, he says, is unlike traditional theory in that it aims to use reality as it presents itself as something more than the starting point for direct imitation: 'The critical acceptance of the categories which rule social life contains simultaneously their condemnation.' ('Traditional and Critical Theory', E p. 219; G p. 157).

In suggesting that we both accept and criticize the given system of categories Horkheimer is evidently drawing on the fourth level of constituting activity to inform the first, epistemological level. It is at the level of the will that the tension shows itself between man as he is and the ideal of a community in which rationality is fully realized. Only in such a community would theory cease to play a two-sided role. Critical Theory has a concept of man 'in conflict with himself' until the opposition between 'the individual's purposefulness, spontaneity and rationality, and the work-process relationships on which society is built' is removed ('Traditional and Critical Theory', E p. 220; G p. 159). This is what sets it its goal in illuminating the concepts in terms of which men know reality: 'Critical Theory in its concept formation and in all phases of its development very consciously makes it own that concern for the rational organization of human activity which it is its task to illumine and legitimate' ('Traditional and Critical Theory', E p. 223; G p. 193).

The assumption that the ideal of rational will can be extended from the fourth level to guide concept formation on the first, epistemological level of activity is a claim which goes beyond the claim that acts of will have a dual character. What warrants the extension of this dual character to guide a conceptual revision of features of reality other than human actions – clouds, trees, animals, etc.? Horkheimer does not say.

Nor does he make it clear what the ideal of rational will is to consist in. He contrasts 'rational self-conscious collective action' with the formal, instrumental rationality characteristic of capitalism. But what does the alternative amount to? Horkheimer, for obvious reasons, cites no contemporary instances of such non-instrumental rationality. Is he really doing anything more materialist than gesturing towards the old romantic doctrine of the harmonious social organism?

Another major question left unresolved in 'Traditional and Critical Theory' is the nature of the superiority claimed for Critical over traditional theory. Does the 'critical acceptance' of received categories imply that Critical Theory aims only to *add* a dimension of understanding neglected by traditional theory, conceding that traditional theory is adequate in its own limited terms? Or does traditional theory fail in even these restricted aims and require replacement?

The question is given point by Horkheimer's choice of Marx's *Critique of Political Economy* as a practical example of Critical Theory. For Marx makes both claims: the reality of the production of value by labour is, he says, obscured by a set of categories (wages, prices, profit) which generate the illusion that the bourgeois order is natural and eternal. But the law of value, once discovered, does not just point *beyond* contemporary society to an alternative economic order; it provides, Marx claims, an empirically superior account of the 'laws of motion' of capitalism itself than any which could be given by political economy which sticks within its 'bourgeois skin'.

Horkheimer, then, does not distinguish the four levels of constituting activity which he makes use of in 'Traditional and Critical Theory' and, by failing to do so, leaves unresolved the important questions arising out of the relationships between them. Subsequent divergences in Critical Theory result from the attempt to make good this omission.

The Negative Dialectic

That Horkheimer should fail to differentiate the four levels of constituting activity was no accident, I suggest, but was encouraged by the fact that all four levels figure together as aspects of a single constituting agency, the *transcendental subject*, in German Idealism. One solution, then, for the problem of the relations between the four levels would be if a materialist equivalent could be found for that Idealist concept. This attempt is made in Theodor Adorno's *Negative Dialectic*, whose grand ambition is no less than to bring together the *Idealist* concept of transcendental subjectivity with the great *sociological* theme of the division of labour.

Written in 1966 it is Adorno's most fully elaborated philosophical work and it is, by any standards, an extremely difficult one. The style is aphoristic and allusive; its goal, as Adorno describes it, is an 'anti-system'. But it would be a grave (if common) mistake to think of the *Negative Dialectic* as a disjointed or inconsistent work – much less as one written in the 'anything-goes (it's all interpretation anyway)' spirit of voguish Nietzscheanism. To the contrary, the *Negative Dialectic* represents the most sustained attempt ever made to work out a consistent Marxist-Hegelian philosophy. Only Lukács's *History and Class Consciousness* approaches its scope, but Adorno's grasp of German Idealist philosophy is incomparably more subtle and profound.

To grasp its implications for the problems left by 'Traditional and Critical Theory' we must first see how the four elements of constitution were related in their original Hegelian context.

Geist (translated sometimes as 'spirit', sometimes as 'mind') is Hegel's version of the transcendental subject. But for Hegel it is not, as he accuses Kant of making it, a quasi-psychological concept. It governs not merely the way that things *appear* to human beings but the way that they are in themselves. Thus, at the ontological level – level (3) – *Geist* is the true source of the identity of the objects encountered in the world – and this not just in virtue of limitations on the way that they can be known. It is an *absolute* subject. But it also underlies the individual's perception of the world, and so fulfils as well the epistemological role played by the transcendental subject in Kant's philosophy – level (1). In the *Phenomenology of Spirit* Hegel traces the process by which these two aspects of *Geist* ('truth' and 'certainty') are brought into coincidence and the stage set for 'absolute knowledge', the subject matter of the *Science of Logic*.

This process of the 'coming-to-itself' of *Geist* also incorporates the other two levels of constitutive activity. It is a concrete historical process (level (2)) – indeed, it is the key to the rational understanding of world history. Men effectively follow the course of *Geist* as they strive to realize ideas whose true identity is not fully disclosed to them; it is this which gives history its rational (in Hegel's sense of the word, *logical*) form.

At the end of history men arrive at a state in which they can act without the identity of their actions escaping them. Political authority in the realized state can be seen to be legitimate – supra-individual but not mysterious. This state is the collective embodiment of rational will – level (4).

Thus *Geist* embodies all four levels of constitution. Adorno's reinterpretation of it has a two-fold structure. There is, first, the aim of 'reading back' the concept of *Geist* in such a way that it becomes apparent that *Geist* is actually an enciphered representation of *society*: 'Beyond the philosophy of identity's magic circle the transcendental subject can be deciphered as society, unconscious of its own self' (*Negative Dialectics*, E p. 177; G p. 179).

But this reinterpretation is not just a direct translation. The 'enciphering' of society in the concept of *Geist* conceals and idealizes what is, in fact, an oppressive feature of capitalist society, namely, the domination of the universal over the particular. It represents as the embodiment of harmony and reconciliation a process which is repressive and antagonistic – an 'order of compulsion':

> The compulsive order of reality, which Idealism projected into the realm of the subject and of *Geist*, is to be translated back out of it. . . . The prior universality [of the process of production] is both true and false: true because it forms that 'ether' which Hegel calls *Geist*; untrue because its 'reason' is, as yet, no such thing, and its universality the product of particular interest.
> (*Negative Dialectics*, E p. 10; G p. 22)

Geist is not, as Idealism would have it, an ontological first cause: the 'ground of grounds'. It is only one pole in a social process cleft between mental and manual labour; a fact which the Idealist illusion of *Geist* as something spontaneous and creative conceals. *Geist's* independence is not original but a *result*, produced by a process of intellectual abstraction corresponding to the regimentation of commodity production: 'Idealism, which distilled [the abstract law-governedness of exchange] into its Absolute Spirit, at once enciphers the truth that the phenomena encounter this mediation in the form of a mechanism of compulsion. *That* is what is concealed behind the so-called problem of constitution'. (*Negative Dialectics*, E p. 47; G p. 57).

This criticism of the Idealist concept of *Geist* means that it cannot function, as it had in Lukács's work, as an affirmative concept, an anticipation of a future, emancipated rational will. The sharpest passages in the *Negative Dialectic* are those in which Adorno exposes Hegel's theodicy of history as a concealed form of authoritarianism. For example:

> The ideology of the independent existence of the Idea is so powerful because it is true. But it is negative truth; it becomes ideology when inverted into affirmation. Once men become aware of the universal's supremacy it is practically inevitable that they should transfigure it, the higher power that they must appease, into *Geist*. They take *force* for *meaning*.
> (*Negative Dialectics*, E p. 315; G p. 310)

However, the difficulties which Adorno's transformation of the concept of *Geist* faces become apparent when one considers its treatment of the material and ontological levels of constitution. As we have seen, these two levels are united in Hegel's system, for all of reality – the material world, as well as human history – is shown to be an embodiment of the absolute, the Idea, whose career is encompassed in the developed structure of the *Begriff* (literally 'concept'). So, according to Hegel, it is wrong to think of concepts having the role of intermediaries, as if they were just the *means* by which human beings come to terms with an essentially mind-independent reality. Concepts (to the extent that they are true) are embodiments of the single *Begriff* which, like the Greek *Logos*, permeates reality and gives it the objective structure which the knowing subject aims at:

> It is an inversion of things to assume that the objects which form
> the content of our ideas come first and that subsequently our
> subjective activity intervenes, forming concepts by the
> aforementioned activity of abstracting and holding together the
> common element in the objects. The *Begriff* is what is truly prior
> and things are what they are by the activity of the *Begriff*,
> immanent and revealing itself in them.
>
> (*Hegel's Logic* (= *Encyclopedia*), para. 163, *Zusatz* 1)

The idea of the immanence of rational structure in the world may be
expressed, Hegel says, by speaking of nature, as Schelling had done,
as 'frozen intelligence'. In nature the Idea is not conscious of itself.
But there is one part of reality which does have this as its aim; human
history is the record of the struggle of *Geist* from immediate consciousness to that point at which it becomes fully aware of its own
nature. The *Begriff* is not just descriptive of *Geist's* structure but
forms the effective *telos* towards which the concrete agents of history
implicitly strive.

Thus both nature – as the Idea 'outside itself' – and history – the
record of its 'coming-to-be in and for itself' – participate in a common
rational structure which founds their intelligibility. Both *material* and
intentional aspects of history are seen to be articulations of a single
process. From the standpoint of philosophical knowledge material
reality can be seen to be adapted to the realization of human purposes,
which are, in turn, inchoate stages in the realization of *Geist*. *Geist* is
the reference point which establishes both the true identity of the
objects we encounter and the final significance of the intentions in
terms of which we act upon them. From this perspective *meaning* and
effective power coincide.

The coincidence is guaranteed for Hegel by the status of *Geist* as an
absolute subject, a claim which Adorno strongly denies. Yet I believe
that, despite its rejection of the Idealist 'primacy of the subject',
Adorno's philosophy itself relies on an assumed coincidence between
history and meaning. This is presupposed by a thesis which I shall call
the objectivity of the meaning process.

It will be recalled that Adorno grants that the career of *Geist*
embodies a real, independent process. What he denies is that this
process can be interpreted affirmatively; the unity of the historical
process is not that of a teleology of self-realization:

Universal history is to be both constructed and denied. . . . The unity which welds together the discontinuous and chaotically fragmented moments and phases of history is undeniable; it is the domination of nature, progressing in the form of domination over man, and, finally, in the domination over their inner nature. (*Negative Dialectics*, E p. 320; G p. 314).

This historical process violates, rather than fulfils, the intrinsic character of whatever forms part of it. Nevertheless, crucially, this is the process to which negative dialectic is to address itself: '[Negative dialectic] accepts unmediated immediacy – the functions which society and its development present to thought – as it comes, in order to release its mediations by analysis, according to the standard of the immanent difference of the phenomena from what they aspire to be in their own right' (*Negative Dialectic*, E p. 38; G p. 48).

The problem, evidently, is to account for how this 'standard' of what phenomena 'aspire to be in their own right' can ever be known. Adorno makes neither of the claims which guarantee for Hegel that the innate significance of historical events is knowable: that history incorporates a movement in which things realize their essence and that we live in an epoch in which historical development has been significantly completed.

Adorno's criticism of Husserl gives an important indication of what his solution to this crucial problem is. Husserl had claimed that the philosopher (suitably initiated by the 'phenomenological reduction') had access to a region in which essential truths could be directly known by what he called an 'intuition of essence'. Adorno, significantly, endorses the idea that such intuition is possible. He seeks, however, to reinterpret it as part of his own theory: the doctrine of the constitutive role of society:

'Intuition of essence' is the name for the physiognomic way of regarding [*Blick auf*] intellectual [*geistige*] matters. It is legitimated by the fact that the intellectual realm is not constituted by the consciousness which is directed towards it cognitively. It is constituted, rather, well beyond the individual who originates it, in the collective life of *Geist*, and is objectively grounded according to its immanent laws.
(*Negative Dialectics*, E p. 82; G p. 89)

Essence, then, is revealed intuitively, *but is objectively grounded in the collective life of Geist*. Here we have, clearly stated, the thesis of the objectivity of meaning. The intuition of essence corresponds to an experience which is, Adorno says, 'the experience of becoming in what, supposedly, merely is' (*Negative Dialectics*, E p. 82; G p. 90). Thus it is the old Idealist category of *werden* (becoming) which carries the link between appearance and essence – between society as it is, and what might be. Philosophy must reveal *becoming* where the course of history serves to obscure it: 'Becoming disappears and dwells in the thing [*Sache*]; as little to be quieted into its own concept as to be split off and forgotten from its result' (*Negative Dialectics*, E p. 52; G p. 62).

Negative dialectic claims to release the history 'congealed in the thing' (*in die Sache geronnen*). Temporal experience is the index according to which to assess reality; a role it is to play despite the fact that it cannot be treated as a stage in the self-realization of the Idea:

> In reading what is as the text of its becoming, Idealist and materialist dialectics are contiguous. But, while Idealism justifies the inner history of immediacy as a stage of the *Begriff*, materialistically it becomes the measure of the untruth of concepts [*Begriffe*] – but, still more, of the untruth of what immediately exists.
> (*Negative Dialectics*, E p. 52; G p. 62)

According to the thesis of the objectivity of meaning, phenomena have an essential significance which is an objective part of the history of the phenomenon itself, and gives it an 'immanent universality': 'Such immanent universality of the individual is objective as sedimented history. . . . To become aware of the constellation in which the object stands is to decipher the history which it bears within itself as something which has become' (*Negative Dialectics*, E p. 163; G p. 165).

As a materialist Adorno denies that natural processes are intrinsically meaningful because nature has a purpose – a *telos* towards which it strives. So what can he mean when he says that history is 'sedimented' in phenomena? How can a materialist say that an object literally 'bears in itself' anything other than a causal natural history? Yet, if Adorno is doing no more than giving metaphorical expression to the idea that men perceive reality in terms of their own purposes and interests, what becomes of the thesis that the meaning process is *objective*?

It is at this point that we see the fundamental equivocation in Adorno's theory. Instead of answering the question of how meaning processes can have this quasi-natural 'objectivity' he slips into an Idealist terminology which conceals the dilemma. Negative dialectic, he says, is to free the 'mediations' which whatever immediately is contains. But what, precisely, is the philosophical status of a 'mediation'? Is it a *causal*, a *logical* or a *semantic* relation? For Hegel, of course, it embraces all three: mediations are 'moments' in the fundamental rational structure of reality. But Adorno, who rejects Hegel's assumption of an absolute subject, has no right to assimilate the three in a way that intimately depends on this assumption. And yet, if he does not, he has no way of explaining the crucial feature of his notion of *Geist*: its ascription to processes of human significance the objectivity usually reserved for material causal processes. Without the quasi-naturalism of the concept of mediation the thesis of the objectivity of the meaning process collapses.

Although the *Negative Dialectic* inverts Idealism, it does not succeed in emancipating itself from it.

Critical Theory without Hegel (1): Knowledge and Human Interests

Inasmuch as it fails to resolve the equivocation in the concept of *Geist* there are objective intellectual reasons why Adorno's philosophy proved a brilliant dead end. Rather than giving an account which could establish the thesis of the objectivity of the meaning process, Adorno's disciples were more concerned to inherit the master's literary-aesthetic nimbus. As a result, to the extent that Critical Theory developed in the nineteen-sixties and seventies, this was entirely the work of Jürgen Habermas.

Habermas's enterprise, however, represents a diametrically opposite approach to the problems left unresolved in 'Traditional and Critical Theory'. Whereas Adorno's reappropriation of the Idealist concept of *Geist* is intended to fuse the *material* and *ontological* levels of constitution into a single, objective process, Habermas concentrates his attention on the *epistemological* level and that of the *rational will*.

As expressed in his major book of the sixties, *Knowledge and Human Interests*, Critical Theory is Kantian rather than Hegelian; not concerned with the nature of reality as it is in itself, but only with the framework which pre-structures men's encounter with it. This framework is *practical* as well as *epistemological* for it conditions both our actions and our knowledge. Thus Habermas emphatically takes up Horkheimer's thesis of epistemological instrumentalism, according to which what we mean by 'reality' is always (only) 'reality as it is for us'. Again, what sets the framework within which we encounter reality is not the transcendental ego, as in Kant, but society – the interests of a historical 'species-subject'.

In this context it is significant that Habermas reads Adorno's work as implying the attribution of meaning to nature: 'The resurrection of nature cannot be logically conceived within materialism, no matter how much the early Marx and the speculative minds in the Marxist tradition (Walter Benjamin, Ernst Bloch, Herbert Marcuse, Theodor W. Adorno) find themselves attracted by the heritage of mysticism' (*Knowledge*, E p. 32; G p. 42).

In fact this is a misreading of Adorno's intentions. Adorno is always careful to distinguish his belief in the objectivity of meaning-processes from an Idealist anthropomorphization of nature. Habermas is assuming that Adorno's conception of *Geist* is untenable and that, as a result, the doctrine of the objectivity of the meaning-process simply collapses back into Idealism. The consequence which he draws from this for his own work is that the search for buried meaning must restrict itself to what is, on Horkheimer's original distinction, the *subjective* side of constitution; philosophy cannot hope to answer ontological questions about reality in itself. He is, for example, quite untroubled by the criticism made by Michael Theunissen (from a standpoint extremely sympathetic to Hegel) that, on such an approach, the objectivity of knowledge becomes 'no more than' *intersubjectivity*. Habermas concedes the point – but sees no criticism in it. (Cf *Knowledge*, E p. 380; G p. 416.)

Habermas follows the tradition of *pragmatism* in believing that the framework for our encounter with reality is historically evolved; the product of the interests of a biological species rather than of a transcendental ego. Two important features separate his 'instrumentalism' from traditional pragmatism, however. In the first place, he rejects any suggestion that the nature of 'interests' can be interpreted from biology alone: 'The concept of "interest" is not meant to imply a naturalistic reduction of transcendental-logical properties to empirical ones. Indeed it is meant to prevent just such a reduction' (*Knowledge*, E p. 196; G p. 241).

Second (and connected with the first point) Habermas claims that we must acknowledge the existence of what German Idealism called an 'interest of reason'; that is to say, that reason itself has independent force and does not require motivating by a non-rational 'passion' in order to be effective: 'In reason there is an inherent drive to realize reason' (*Knowledge*, E p. 201; G p. 248).

The true interests of the species are not simply the biological ones derived from self-preservation; they are for the species to develop itself into a rational, autonomous community. To do so it must achieve self-knowledge by reappropriating its own activity (a process which Habermas calls *reflection*) in structuring reality. In this way philosophy and history are brought together. As the species becomes aware of its own accomplishments its capacity for rational action is enhanced. At the level of the species epistemological progress co-incides with the formation of a rational will.

By concentrating on the epistemological side of constitution and the formation of a rational will *Knowledge and Human Interests* develops a conception of Critical Theory which risks none of the dubious theses of Idealist ontology. But it must rely heavily on the thesis of epis-temological instrumentalism. There are, I think, decisive objections to this thesis.

At the root of these objections lies the difficulty of determining the instrumentalist thesis's philosophical status – a difficulty which arises in great measure from the fact that it is formulated in opposition to a position which is itself ambiguous. This position embodies what Habermas terms 'the illusion of objectivism': the belief that our perception reflects reality as it is in itself.

Now in its classic, empiricist form *objectivism* in fact incorporates two sorts of claim; *psychological* and *metaphysical*. On the level of psychology it asserts that our perceptual apparatus plays an essentially passive role, simply registering on the '*tabula rasa*' of the mind whatever reality happens to inscribe there. But because of this we are entitled to assert a further, overarching metaphysical thesis: the per-ception we have corresponds to the way the world is in itself.

It is, indeed, easy to challenge the naive theory of perception on which such classical objectivism is based. As cognitive psychologists have been showing for at least a hundred years our purportedly *direct* reception of reality is, in fact, informed in ways of which we are not aware by 'interpretations'. The tenacity of perceptual illusions is one conclusive demonstration that perceptions, towards which, as far as our own awareness goes, we are entirely passive, in fact can be said to incorporate the subject's activity.

But what follows from conceding this? If the findings of cognitive psychology refute the first of the two claims made by classical objectivism – the thesis of passive perception – does it then follow that the thesis of the correspondence between mind and world is also refuted? No: logically, although the metaphysical thesis is *supported* by the psychological one, it does not itself depend on it. All that one can say is that, if the psychological thesis is false, the metaphysical thesis requires establishment on other grounds.

The findings of cognitive psychology, although they can refute the thesis of passive perception, in no way imply a contrary metaphysical thesis. As Kant's followers (Husserl, for one) have pointed out, the question of man's relation to the world is a *transcendental* question to which the deliverances of an empirical science like cognitive psychology are epistemologically posterior. Cognitive psychology frames its theories, after all, in a language which assumes the independent existence of the entities to which it refers. It already presupposes an objective world.

This is not a conclusive objection to instrumentalism, for it is open to the defender of instrumentalism to reply that he is using the findings of cognitive psychology in order to make something other than a *transcendental* claim, in Kant's or Husserl's sense: a thesis about the overarching relations between mind and world. But what does the instrumentalist thesis amount to if it is *not* a transcendental thesis?

It cannot be an empirical one, for, as an empirical thesis, it lacks sufficient precision to be informative. To say that we live in a world constituted by the activity of knowing subjects is informative only if we have some means to determine that activity's extent: how the balance is struck between *active* and *passive* components in perception. But this, of course, the instrumentalist can never have without assuming what, in giving up his transcendental claim, he has denied himself: some vantage point outside our everyday knowledge of the world from which to resolve perception into the *matter* received by the senses and the *form* imposed on it. Kant thought that he could draw the distinction on *a priori* grounds. Habermas, however, leaves the problem at the level of an antithesis: 'We cannot meaningfully conceive of anything like uninterpreted facts. Yet the facts cannot be exhaustively reduced to our interpretation' (*Knowledge*, E p. 97; G p. 124).

But, in the absence of a standpoint from which this element in 'facts' which resists being 'reduced to our interpretations' could be isolated, the antithesis is empirically meaningless, and Habermas's instrumentalism turns back, willy-nilly, into an uninformative transcendental claim.

Critical Theory without Hegel (2): Communication and the Evolution of Society

Perhaps it is an implicit acknowledgement of these difficulties that instrumentalist epistemology plays a much less prominent role in Habermas's recent work. In *Communication and the Evolution of Society* (1976) it has receded in favour of a claim about *social meaning*: the structure which the philosopher aims to disclose is not now the effect of *interest* on men's encounter with the world and each other but the *rules* which they must follow in order to perform significant social actions. (The two claims are not, however, logically incompatible, so it would be premature to say that Habermas has rejected instrumentalism.)

Society, Habermas defines as a 'symbolically prestructured segment of reality' (*Communication*, p. 66), in the sense that the identity of specifically social phenomena is fixed according to a network of rules. This is a claim on the third, ontological level of constitution. But it is not – in contrast to Hegel – a claim about the ultimate being of phenomena. It concerns only that segment of reality which human beings endow with significance: that which is subject to *conventions* (*Communication*, p. 35). Society, in the sense defined, is open to 'communicative understanding' and philosophy has the task of making explicit ('reconstructing') what that understanding consists in: the grasp of the rules which underlie a symbolic structure: 'The interpreter attempts to explicate the meaning of a symbolic formation in terms of the rules according to which the author must have brought it forth. . . . He attempts . . . to peer through the surface, as it were, and into the symbolic formation to discover the rules according to which the latter was produced' (*Communication*, p. 12).

Evidently, the equation of *meaning* with *production according to rules* is crucial. It guarantees that what is meaningful is, at least in principle, an object of systematic knowledge (rather than something just lived and experienced intuitively). Thus it is surprising and damaging that Habermas offers no defence of the thesis; the more so because in both the German and the Anglo-Saxon traditions powerful voices have been raised in objection to it.

For an example of opposition to the equation of meaning and rules in the German tradition we need only return to Adorno. Adorno's objection (which has its ancestry in Kant) is that to equate meaning with rules is to restrict the nature of judgement to a formal procedure of classification. If the meaning of a concept can be expressed in a rule then the application of the concept in judgement need be no more than the subsumption of experience under that rule. In that case, however, whatever is specific or qualitative about experience – the non-identical, in Adorno's terminology – passes beyond the scope of knowledge. The restriction of what is knowable to what can be formally classified is, Adorno asserts, a fallacy, although one with a basis in social reality: it is a mental correlative to the abstract order of commodity production: 'The individual is more, as well as less, than its universal determination. . . . The contradiction between universal and particular has the significance that individuality does not yet exist' (*Negative Dialectics*, E p. 151; G p. 154).

Philosophy – here Adorno is at one with his arch-enemy, Heidegger – in trying to give conceptual expression to what is dissonant and unclassifiable, becomes contiguous with art. The work of art is a paradigm in that it has a coherent internal structure (Adorno talks of 'submitting to its discipline') but, because it is non-conceptual, escapes the mutilating effects of classification.

But objection to the equation of meaning and rules is by no means restricted to these German anti-positivists. The burgeoning discussion in the Anglo-Saxon countries shows this. This discussion has a different starting-point, however: Wittgenstein's familiar (if still controversial) considerations on rule-following in the *Philosophical Investigations*.

It is common ground among interpreters that Wittgenstein starts his discussion from the claim that a formulated body of rules is insufficient to specify the course of a systematic practice, such as applying a word. What is controversial, however, is whether Wittgenstein is using this claim as part of an attack on the notion that meaning is governed by rules, or not. Peter Winch's *The Idea of a*

Social Science has been the most influential statement of the view that Wittgenstein supports the equation of meaning and rules, and it is my assumption that Habermas relies on Winch's interpretation of Wittgenstein for his own rules thesis.

Winch argues that the insufficiency of rule formulations is a problem for the *identification* of the rules being employed, not an argument against their existence: 'What is the difference between someone who is really applying a rule in what he does and someone who is not? . . . [That] a man's action *might* be interpreted as an application of a given formula is in itself no guarantee that he is in fact applying that formula' (*The Idea of a Social Science*, p. 29).

We can know independently of observation that language use *must* be governed by rules, Winch says, for without them we should lack the standards to determine whether, on any two occasions, we were saying and meaning the same thing. If the practices we carry out can be expressed by more than one rule formulation then this only means that it is not possible to identify which rule is being followed by inspection of the course of the practice alone; the rule must be part of a 'form of life' on the part of the community, which fixes the rule being employed.

That Wittgenstein rejects the equation of meaning and rules has been asserted no less vigorously, however; Stanley Cavell, for example, is vehement in his denial of the rules thesis. Cavell says that 'whether the later Wittgenstein describes language as being roughly like a calculus with fixed rules . . . is not a question that can be seriously discussed' (*Must We Mean What We Say?*, p. 48); all of Wittgenstein's later work is directed against just this conception. Wittgenstein 'wishes to indicate how inessential the "appeal to rules" is as an explanation of language' (*Must We Mean What We Say?*, p. 52).

I think that both logic and (although I do not have the space to argue this here) Wittgenstein's text support Cavell. In order to demonstrate this it is helpful to differentiate the rather general claim that rule formulations fail to specify a practice into two theses which I shall call the *underdetermination* thesis and the *overdetermination* thesis.

The underdetermination thesis argues that the reason why systems of rules fail to specify practices is that no system of rules can, in principle, be rich enough to include all the circumstances of its application. The argument is close to Adorno's and also goes back to

Kant. Take a rule of standard form: 'In circumstances A_1 . . . A_n do (or say)*phi*'; or 'In circumstances A_1 . . . A_n X counts as Y'. How does one determine whether the circumstances stated as conditions for the rule's application obtain? To answer that one determines the existence of A_1 . . . A_n by rules for their identification evidently leads to a regress, for those identifying rules will themselves require specification, and so on. The underdetermination thesis either refutes the claim that meaning is governed by rules or renders it trivial. It refutes the claim if it is part of that claim that the rules said to govern our practice must be capable of non-circular specification, for it shows that all rules have limits to their specification which rules alone cannot transcend. It renders the claim quite trivial if we deny that such a specification is necessary. In that case it would be permissible to give as rules of language use rules of the sort: 'Call all and only those things "red" which are red' – rules which, though undeniable, are explanatorily empty.

The overdetermination thesis is as follows: Any practice is composed of a finite sequence of separate performances, and may be expressed in a variety of different rule formulations. We may think, for example, that a sequence of numbers has been formed according to the rule 'add two'. But that is only one possible formulation; it is always possible that when a new element is added to the sequence we will find that we were wrong and that the sequence corresponds to some – but, importantly, not just to *one* – different formulation.

Although I think that Wittgenstein uses both theses, Winch only treats the second, overdetermination thesis. It is clear, however, that the underdetermination thesis, if accepted, is fatal to Winch's position. The community, according to Winch, is involved in *settling* which of the various rules on offer is the one which is, in fact, being applied. But the underdetermination thesis sets the problem as that of continuing a sequence in circumstances past the point at which rules are informative; there is no help to be had in choosing *between* rules where rules no longer extend. Thus the appeal to the community can only be a defence against the overdetermination thesis.

But, even restricting consideration exclusively to the overdetermination thesis, Winch's argument is inadequate. According to Wittgenstein a variety of rule formulations can be given for a sequence *at any stage*. Now imagine that at some stage the community takes a particular continuation. Does this settle the question of which rule it is following? No. No single 'decision' can ever do this because, by assumption, at the next stage of the sequence *precisely the same problem will arise*. Once again several rule formulations will apply and the community's previous 'decision' will be insufficient to settle which one is 'truly' being applied. The point of Wittgenstein's argument is that it is not possible for the community to fix *the* rule being employed. All it can do is agree that this or that continuation is the right one at a particular stage. It cannot settle on a rule formulation and then, as it were, sit back and let things take their course, as if guided by 'infinitely long rails' (*Philosophical Investigations* I, 218). Rules do not explain why we can continue (some) practices as a matter of course. We just can.

The argument against the equation of meaning with rules leads to a textual point with important wider implications. Winch bases his claim for the necessary existence of rules governing meaning on the argument that rules are indispensable in order to establish the identity of meanings. This is how we know that there must be rules. He quotes the connection which Wittgenstein makes between the existence of rules and our ability to use the word 'same':

> [The] question: What is it for a word to have a meaning? leads on to the question: What is it for someone to follow a rule? . . . We should like to say: someone is following a rule if he always acts in the same way on the same kind of occasion. But this again, though correct, does not advance matters since, as we have seen, it is only in terms of a given rule that the word 'same' acquires a definite sense. 'The use of the word "rule" and the use of the word "same" are interwoven. (As are the use of "proposition" and the use of "true")' (*Philosophical Investigations I*, 225).
> (*The Idea of a Social Science*, p. 28)

Wittgenstein undeniably relates *identity* of meaning to the existence of rules. But it is wrong to take this to imply that the existence of meaning presupposes the existence of rules without giving consideration to the opposite possibility: that there may be *meaning* without *identity of meaning*. Winch asserts so frequently in the course of his book that there 'must' be standards to establish that we are saying the same thing on different occasions that it is easy to ignore the fact that the only argument he gives is circular: without such standards there would be nothing to *guarantee* that we are using a word in the unique correct way (*The Idea of a Social Science*, pp. 25–9). But why must there be such a guarantee? Why must a sharp line exist to divide 'correct' from 'incorrect' usage?

Must we always, for instance, be able to distinguish, on pain of meaninglessness or ambiguity, between whether the application of a word in a new context represents a *continuation* or a *change* in meaning? Is the word 'strong' being used with its original meaning when we predicate it of a chain or a cup of tea but with a new one when said of a musical performance or an assumption? If meaning is not a matter of fixed rules is there any reason to assume that it is a matter of fixed identity either? Winch's argument could, in fact, be turned around: the fact that there are cases in which the question of 'old' or 'new' meaning is unanswerable casts doubt on any doctrine which entails that a boundary between the two *must* exist.

This radical conclusion draws Wittgenstein towards a reiterated claim of continental philosophy since the romantics: the impossibility of fixing a rigid dividing line between literal ('cognitive') and metaphorical ('poetic') discourse. If no rules fix the literal meanings of words who is to say that the scientist remains soberly within their limits while the poet licentiously transgresses them?

Conventionalism

With the dispute over the equation of meaning and rules Critical Theory comes full circle. No longer is it a matter of dealing with issues quite different from those preoccupying the Anglo-Saxon world; the dispute over rules actually divides both traditions. To challenge Habermas's use of the equation of meaning and rules is also to criticize, by implication, a broad stream of Anglo-Saxon philosophy. For not only is the equation stated expressly in such important works as *The Idea of a Social Science* and John Searle's *Speech Acts*, it is a presupposition of many others. (According to John McDowell, for example, it is an assumption in both Michael Dummett's approach to the theory of meaning and Richard Hare's analysis of moral discourse.)

The equation of meaning and rules is so widespread – and so little supported by explicit argument – as to suggest that it is, in Wittgenstein's terms, a philosophical *picture*: a view which, though explanatorily empty, nevertheless grips philosophers with its vividness and appeal to 'common sense'. But common sense, as Gramsci remarks, is the practical wisdom of the ruling class, and the ideological function of the equation of meaning and rules is not hard to identify: it gives crucial support to a view of social meaning as essentially a matter of *convention*.

To appreciate this it is necessary to distinguish between a broad and a narrow sense of convention. In the broad sense convention is simply a general term for those features of reality which are essentially social in character: *nomoi* rather than *physei*, as the Greek philosophers put it. (This, I believe, is the sense in which Wittgenstein sometimes speaks of meaning as a matter of convention; in the stronger sense Wittgenstein was not a conventionalist.) But a more restricted sense of convention is now common. In this sense conventions are specifically agreements or undertakings: that in such-and-such circumstances an X is a Y (a two of clubs is a trump) or a *phi* is done (a point scored). Conventionalism is the doctrine that all social meanings are conventions in this second, narrow sense.

The immediately obvious objection to conventionalism is this: No one could claim that all social meanings are a matter of explicit agreement. But if agreement is, at most, only tacit, what becomes of its binding force? The objection is illuminating to the extent that it makes apparent the role which the equation of meaning and rules plays for conventionalism. It is not, the conventionalist will reply, that social meanings are conventional in the sense of having the binding force of explicitly made agreements. What they have in common with explicit agreements is their form: the form of *rules*.

This is the claim advanced in John Searle's *Speech Acts*. In that book Searle defends 'the distinction between brute and institutional facts' (p. 50), the distinction between facts which are the objects of natural science and those which are objects of social understanding: '[Institutional facts] are indeed facts; but their existence, unlike the existence of brute facts, presupposes the existence of certain human institutions. . . . These 'institutions' are systems of constitutive rules. *Every institutional fact is underlain by a (system of) rule[s] of the form "X counts as Y in context C"* ' (*Speech Acts*, p. 51, my emphasis).

Not the least objectionable feature of conventionalism is this presentation of it as the sole alternative to scientific reductionism. We must either, it is said, acknowledge that social meanings are institutional facts, or accept the assimilation of the social sciences to the sciences of nature. It is: nature *or* convention.

Conventionalism is not confined to philosophers, either. Its assumptions vitiate the work of so distinguished a social theorist as Mary Douglas. In the introduction to her collection *Rules and Meanings* she writes:

> There is a recognizable epistemological viewpoint, working through European literature, philosophy, linguistics and sociology which strikes some students as novel when they meet it. . . .
> A conversation started in Europe between philosophers and social scientists. . . . [The speakers] knew only too well that there can be rules without meaning. *They also assumed that there can be no meaning without rules.* . . . But once begun, this conversation, so hopeful of solving epistemological problems, soon split up into the musings of diverse specialists. *As a result, our knowledge of the social conventions which made understanding possible remains scarcely advanced from that beginning. . . . The theme goes back to Hegel and Marx; that reality is socially constructed.*
> (*Rules and Meanings*, p. 9, my emphasis)

The speculative history of ideas displayed in this passage embodies a confusion. As the emphasized sentences show, Douglas characterizes her 'conversation' in three distinct ways. Its participants believed: (1) 'that there can be no meaning without rules'; (2) that 'social conventions make understanding possible'; and (3) 'that reality is socially constructed'. Yet these three theses are not equivalent and to treat them as three versions of the rules thesis leads to historical absurdity; Hegel and Marx may have believed that reality is socially constructed (constituted would have been more accurate), but conventionalists they never were. The unquestioned assumption of conventionalism makes Douglas's approach, its cosmopolitan tone notwithstanding, unexpectedly parochial.

Conclusion

The view that the social origin of meaning is to be found in tacitly acknowledged conventions is, thus, only one – characteristically English – response to reductionism about meaning. There is a quite different, characteristically German, response which seeks the origin of meaning in the constituting activity of a transcendental subject or *Geist*. Both have been represented in Critical Theory for both can be accommodated to its vision of philosophy as an emancipatory force bringing men to self-understanding.

But there is another, third, response to reductionism which is, if my reading is correct, Wittgenstein's. This is the view that social meaning is autonomous, in the sense that there is *no* point of origin to which meanings can be referred back. The significance of Wittgenstein's famous question – what gives life to a system of signs? – is that it is, in an important sense, unanswerable. To answer it would be to fall back into the search for an agency behind the system. We can, however, neither trace meanings back to natural processes, nor refer them to a founding spirit (or system of rules). As Goethe puts it: '*Man suche nur nichts hinter den Phänomenen: sie selbst sind die Lehre.*'

Yet where would this leave Critical Theory? Can this conception, too, be made part of a philosophy with a contribution to make in human beings' search for rational self-understanding? These are important questions, but lack of space – and lack of answers – prevent me from pursuing them here.

5

The Prescription is Description: Wittgenstein's View of the Human Sciences

Theodore R. Schatzki

Wittgenstein's view on the nature and task of philosophy have been immensely influential in this century. They are largely responsible, for instance, for the type of philosophy called 'Ordinary Language Philosophy' that flourished at Oxford during the fifties and sixties. The method that Wittgenstein proposes for philosophy involves the careful description of the phenomena involved in and surrounding human action. He also recommends that a formally identical descriptive method be used by the interpretative human sciences (sciences whose goal is to make actions and practices intelligible). Because the type of method used by a discipline is greatly determined by the type of understanding it seeks, the following question naturally arises: in what ways is the type of understanding that Wittgenstein thinks philosophy should seek similar to the type of understanding that he thinks interpretative human science does seek? In view of the fact that recent debate about the foundations of the human sciences has often centered on the interpretative nature of particular disciplines within this field, I think that it will be of some interest to become clear about what Wittgenstein thinks about their interpretative nature and why.[1] This is especially true because Wittgenstein has been used by writers such as P. Winch and K.O. Apel[2] as a participant in this debate in ways I think are incorrect.

Before beginning, it is important to understand the peculiar difficulties facing any writer on Wittgenstein. His work, on the whole, appears to be a somewhat disordered collection of simple remarks, on a wide variety of subjects, whose individual significance and mutual relevance is often unclear – he himself calls them a collection of 'sketches' (*PI*, preface).[3] In sharp contrast to practically all written philosophy, there are almost no general conclusions, and statements that sound like conclusions often have an enigmatic character. Further, there are few statements explaining what he is doing and why he is doing it. One exception to this are the places, notably in one section of the *Philosophical Investigations*, where Wittgenstein makes relatively explicit and general remarks about the nature of philosophy and the characteristics of his own approach to philosophical problems. His comments, however, remain somewhat cryptic, and to understand what, at bottom, generates his vision and methodological recommendations, we must look elsewhere. Similarly, although Wittgenstein's explicit remarks about interpretative human sciences appear, for the most part, in two short pieces ('Remarks on Frazer's *Golden Bough*' and 'Conversations with Freud'), what motivates, and in the end rationalizes what he says there can be discovered only by studying remarks that are scattered throughout his work.

Because of the fragmented character of Wittgenstein's statements, an interpreter must delve beneath their surface and attempt to uncover the presuppositions and ideas which unify and make them intelligible. The result of this process is that one might attribute theses to Wittgenstein's work with which he would have disagreed (if one had asked him). This does not mean, however, that one is illegitimately reading them into his work. The meaning and unity of a text can, and often does, outrun the intentions, thoughts, and self-conceptions of its author, because what lies implicitly and unbeknownst to the author in the text can both contribute to its meaning and be a part of the vision animating the work. Therefore, it is not the word of the author that decides whether given ideas underlie his writings, but the degree to which they are able to unify and make the text intelligible.

Phenomenology of the Everyday

Because Wittgenstein is more explicit about his views on philosophy than on interpretative science, it is best to begin with a discussion of the nature of philosophical problems and his recommendation about how to resolve them.

A philosopher, for Wittgenstein, is anyone concerned with the questions that philosophers have traditionally asked. These questions fall into two classes. Questions that belong to the first class – nearly all philosophical problems[4] – are 'illegitimate' according to Wittgenstein. This is because asking them is possible only if one first makes a mistake. He considers questions in the second class, questions of essence – What is thought?, What is truth?, What is beauty? – legitimate. The philosophical tradition, however, had made a mistake in attempting to provide *theoretical* solutions to them. For Wittgenstein, the only way to approach philosophical problems is to *dissolve* them by analysing concepts through the description of the everyday use of language.

The mistakes that Wittgenstein attributes to the philosophical tradition have two components. The first is a direct misunderstanding of language. Examples of this are the assimilation of expressions occurring in one area of discourse to expressions occurring in another (*PI* 40; = the assimilation of concepts used in different domains of discourse) and the invention of non-existent referents for words that look like referring expressions. The particular misunderstanding that underlies the theoretical approach to questions of essence is the assumption that there is something common to everything that falls under a particular general term (*BB* 17; = the assumption that there is something common to all instances of a given concept). The second component of the mistake is that these misunderstandings encourage the uncritical acceptance of a 'picture' of the way things must be, a picture that is usually incorrect because it is not developed through research. (It is important to realize that Wittgenstein is not against 'pictures' *per se* – only incorrect ones.)

Wittgenstein offers the following example of the genesis of an illegitimate philosophical problem: 'Augustine . . . argued: "How is it possible that one should measure time? For the past can't be measured, as it is gone by, and the future can't be measured because it has not yet come. And the present can't be measured for it has no extension" ' (*BB* 26). Augustine, Wittgenstein argues, has misunderstood the concept of (the expression) 'measuring time'. Because he assimilates it to the concept of (the expression) 'measuring length', just as one measures length by holding a ruler up to an object, he pictures the measurement of time as holding a ruler up to a conveyor belt that constantly passes before one and that one can see only a tiny stretch of at any given moment. This 'picture' then gives birth to the following paradox, a philosophical problem: How can one measure any distance on this conveyor belt when one can see only a single point on it? That is: How is it possible to measure time? This problem, however, arises only from a picture itself based on the faulty assimilation of two concepts. If Augustine got clear about the concept of measuring time, he would not assimilate it to the concept of measuring length, and the picture and accompanying problem would never arise.

An example of the way philosophers attempt to answer the question, What is thought?, is to revert to a theory of mind which either specifies the elements of thought and how they combine, or explains how the activities of the mind interact with other mental and non-mental entities. Here, Wittgenstein suggests, the philosopher makes the assumption that all the phenomena called thinking (all instances of thinking) have something in common – that they are cases of mental activity. The philosopher then constructs a theory, based on a particular picture of what the mind is, that attempts to account for and build upon this common element. But, Wittgenstein points out, if one analyses the concept of thinking, one discovers that not all the phenomena called cases of thinking are phenomena of mental activity. So the philosopher's answer to his question is based on a misunderstanding. The question, What is thought?, is a legitimate question, but the answer to it can come only at the conclusion of an examination of the concept of thought.[5]

Philosophical problems, therefore, arise because the philosopher misunderstands concepts. But he does not realize this. The philosopher does not realize that he is in the grip of a picture, because he misunderstands language *before* beginning to philosophize. The problem, Wittgenstein writes, is that we normally lack a 'clear view of the use of our words' (*PI* 122; why this is so I will explain later). Lacking such a view, and unaware that he lacks it, the philosopher inevitably falls prey to the misunderstandings that underlie philosophical questions such as he asks them.

True philosophy is a kind of therapy. Quite unintentionally, the philosopher has contracted a 'disease of the mind', whose overt manifestations are asking (mostly) bad questions and incorrectly answering the rest. Wittgenstein thinks that his method of doing philosophy, by treating the root of this disease – misunderstandings – can cure it. ('Philosophy is the clearing away of misunderstandings, nonsense, and the bumps of the understanding' (*PI* 119).) If it succeeds, the symptoms will disappear – the philosopher will no longer raise philosophical questions and he will use Wittgenstein's method to answer questions of essence. The end result is that the philosopher, no longer tormented by his problems, feels at ease with himself and his work. Wittgenstein once described himself as a disciple of Freud (*LC* 41), and one can discern the influence of the latter on this conception of philosophy.

So the type of understanding one seeks in philosophy is an understanding of concepts. To reveal the nature of this understanding, I must discuss the method Wittgenstein proposes for analysing concepts. Concepts, for him, are the grounds on which we organize phenomena into interwoven patterns of similarity and dissimilarity. They are grounds of classification (*RFM* II/14). The dominant way in which we classify phenomena is via the use of language (there is no implication that this is the only function of language). Consider the word 'thinking'. In calling many phenomena cases of thinking, we thereby classify them as instances of this type of activity. An example of such a phenomenon is, while in the act of writing, testing the point of one's pen, making a face, and going on with a gesture of resignation (*PI* 330). The ground of this classification, the ground of this and this and this being called cases of thinking, is the concept of thinking. Wittgenstein thus writes that a concept is something like a picture with which one compares objects (*RFM* V/50) in order to decide if the objects are instances of what is represented therein.

When we form a new concept, say the concept of 'rapsmonk', we now have a new ground of classification; that is, we now call this and this and this cases of rapsmonk where before nothing was so called. Accordingly, changes in the concept of rapsmonk, changes in the ground of the classification that consists in calling various phenomena rapsmonk, are expressed by changes in *which* phenomena we call rapsmonk (*RFM* III/29). How, then, does one uncover this ground?

Clearly the best way to uncover it is to describe cases of rapsmonk and to try to discover what it is in virtue of which they are instances of this concept. (This will involve, for instance, filling out the context of the occasions on which rapsmonk is ascribed to something.) Wittgenstein thinks, however, that there is no element common to all instances of (at least, but not only) those concepts that philosophers have traditionally been interested in – truth, thought, knowledge, goodness, justice, life etc. Instances of any such concept form a large, varied family which are individually similar to and different from each other in various ways (much like the faces of the members of a single family, which resemble and differ from one another in diverse ways while remaining somehow alike (cf *PI* 67)). There is, Wittgenstein writes, no 'red thread' running through them all, only a mass of overlapping fibres. So there is no single attribute in virtue of which all cases of, say, thinking, qualify as instances of this concept. If so, what makes them all cases of thinking?

The answer is that there is nothing that *makes* them cases of thinking. There is no verbally formalizable reason or rule why we call just these phenomena, and not others, cases of thinking – this is simply what we do (on the other hand, there might be a *cause* of our so acting). Nevertheless, the phenomena of thinking do have a particular physiognomy (cf *Z* 376; *RFM* V/14) – just as the faces of members of a single family have a particular physiognomy. And by describing phenomena called cases of thinking and the contexts in which they occur, arranging such descriptions in a manner which allows one to pass easily from one case to another (thereby attaining a clear view of their interrelations), one gradually comes to understand this physiognomy and to see *what thinking is*. (For Wittgenstein, understanding the concept of X is identical to understanding what X is (cf *RFM* I/73).) But it is not possible to describe this physiognomy or to say what thinking is. So the type of understanding sought in philosophy, the understanding of concepts, is inexpressible in words. The only way to communicate this understanding to someone who does not yet possess it is to give him examples of thinking and hope that he 'catches on'. (He shows that he understands when he can use the word 'thinking' as we all do.)

Now Wittgenstein writes that one elucidates the concept of thinking by attaining a 'surveyable (*übersichtlichen*) representation' (*PI* 122) of the use of the word 'thinking' (*PI* 383; the clear view of the use of our words that the traditional philosopher lacked). This is so because it is the use of the word 'thinking', in descriptions of phenomena and ascriptions of thinking to oneself and others, that designates certain phenomena as cases of thinking. Hence describing the use of the word consists primarily in describing these phenomena; and thus attaining an *übersichtlichen* representation of this use involves attaining an *übersichtlichen* representation of these phenomena.

It is interesting to see how the type of understanding sought in philosophy is related to the practical understanding of how to use words. In learning to speak a language, one acquires an ability to recognize the phenomena to which particular general terms can be descriptively and ascriptively applied. Hence philosophy can be seen as an attempt to make this practical understanding explicit. As I've explained, Wittgenstein thinks that this attempt can have, at best, limited success. It should also be mentioned that an important aspect of Wittgenstein's method is describing imaginary situations and seeing if one would intuitively call them cases of, e.g., thinking. Here one utilizes one's practical understanding of the word 'think' to test whether something qualifies as a case of thinking. This is an important aspect of the method, because one can choose how to construct the examples. By skilfully doing this, one might be able to collect an array of imaginary phenomena of thinking, or an array of both actual and imaginary such phenomena, that is more effective than an array of actual phenomena alone in leading one to see the physiognomy belonging to all possible cases of thinking.[6]

Let us return to Augustine and examine the treatment Wittgenstein prescribes for him. If Augustine had described the use of the expressions 'measuring time' and 'measuring length', and thereby examined cases of both measuring time and measuring length, he would have realized that he had assimilated the concept of measuring time to the concept of measuring length. Once he had understood how different the two concepts are, then not only would the faulty conveyor-belt picture of measuring time never have arisen, or at least never have gained credence, but there would have been no temptation to ask the philosophical question, How is it possible to measure time?, because this question can be raised only if the assimilation is made and the picture adopted. In fact, by examining cases of measuring time, Augustine would have seen how it is done and hence how it is possible.

Similarly, Wittgenstein prescribes a heavy dose of description to the philosopher who assumes that there is something common to all cases of knowledge and constructs a theory to answer the question, What is knowledge? Once this philosopher sees that the phenomena called cases of knowledge form a complex collection whose members share no particular feature, he understands his mistake and realizes that in order to grasp what knowledge is, he must acquire an overview of this collection. For this purpose, a theory is clearly useless. Any attempt to reduce the manifold of knowledge-phenomena to variations on archetypes or combinations of theoretical parameters only hides its complexity. Moreover, such an attempt buries the individual characteristics of each of the cases of knowledge, the appreciation of which is what leads one to an understanding of the physiognomy of knowledge.

In this way, Wittgenstein prescribes a method for philosophers which by describing phenomena called (cases of) X elucidates the concept of X and enables one to see what X is. Hence, it is a form of both conceptual and essential analysis. I would like to call Wittgenstein's method, 'Phenomenology of the Everyday', because what a practitioner does is describe the phenomena of everyday, i.e. non-philosophical, life. It might be a bit of a let-down to the philosopher to discover that he is supposed to describe 'mundane' states of affairs, but this is the price, Wittgenstein might say, of asking the questions he does.

I have now examined the method Wittgenstein proposes for philosophy and the nature of the understanding it is supposed to achieve. Although I have gone some distance toward explaining why Wittgenstein thought that his method was the true path for philosophy, the whole story has not yet been told. It has not yet been explained why it is so easy to misunderstand language, and it is possible to throw more light on the idea that the description of word-use elucidates concepts. These promissory notes will be cashed shortly, but first it is necessary to consider an as yet undiscussed aspect of Wittgenstein's method and to talk a bit about the goal of the interpretative sciences of man.

Wittgenstein's technical terms

Wittgenstein provides a set of technical terms to guide the type of description he proposes. These technical terms are 'form of life', 'language-game', 'rule', 'grammar', and 'criterion'. I call them 'technical', not because they are used in a theory or hypothesis about anything, but because Wittgenstein employs them for the purpose of suggesting a new way of looking at language. He advances this new way because only if one looks at language from a novel perspective will one adopt his method of doing philosophy. These terms thus play three roles: they characterize language in a novel way, and in so doing, make Phenomenology of the Everyday plausible and direct one in performing it.

Wittgenstein writes: 'The term "language-game" is meant to bring into prominence the fact that the *speaking* of the language is part of an activity . . .' (*PI* 23). A language-game consists both of the use of a particular element of language (word, expression, sentence, etc.) and of features of the activities in which instances of that use are embedded. For example, the language-game with the word 'knowledge' consists of the linguistic actions in which it figures (assertions, descriptions, questions etc.) and those aspects of the activities of which these linguistic actions are a part that either lead up to, accompany, are affected by, or referred to by the use of this word. So when describing this language-game one would describe the situations in which the word 'knowledge' (and cognates) is used, what is said by the linguistic actions involved, the effect it has on other people, what it refers to (if used referringly), the reasons why it is used, its influence on the course of the activity, and so on. The term 'language-game' is meant to remind us of the fact that speaking a language is nothing but one functional element among others in human activities, albeit a rather special one.

The term 'form of life' refers to the totality of practices, activities, and ways of being in which a person, or a group of people, is able to participate in virtue of becoming a member of a particular social organization. So when Wittgenstein completes the above quotation, 'The term "language-*game*" is meant to bring into prominence the fact that the *speaking* of the language is part of an activity, or of a form of life', he brings out the fact that the use of language is one element among many in our activities, which themselves are embedded in a matrix of interrelated actual and possible activities, the totality of which constitutes the form of life in which the user of language finds himself.

When Wittgenstein suggests that all behaviour can be described as 'rule-governed', he uses 'rule' in the sense of a 'natural law . . . describing the behaviour of . . .' people (*BB* 98). Wittgenstein distinguishes between two primary senses of the word 'rule' (*BB* 13). In one sense of the word, a rule is an instruction consulted or referred to in the performance of action. It is with this sense of 'rule' that we speak of an 'expression of a rule' (*BB* 95) being 'involved in a process' (*BB* 13). Here it is the rule that determines what one does and not *vice versa*. On the other hand, a rule in the sense in which all behaviour can be described as 'rule-governed' is not an element in the behaviour, something that determines that behaviour goes this way but not that. Rather, a rule is a description of a regularity in behaviour, however that regularity is caused. Here, it is the behaviour that determines the rule and not *vice versa* – the behaviour is 'in accordance with' a rule only in the sense that a rule can be formulated that adequately represents the regularity in behaviour. So no causal properties are ascribed to this second kind of rule; citing them are our ways of *ex post facto* describing our behaviour.

In claiming that all language-use can be described as 'rule-governed', Wittgenstein suggests that language-use is composed of regularities that can be described in terms of rules. It is important to realize that there is no unique set of rules that we 'follow' in our behaviour. Because rules, in the sense of the word in which all practices are rule-governed, are not what make us do what we do, there is no set of rules that are the rules we *in fact* follow. Furthermore, because there are alternative sets of rules that equally well describe regularities in linguistic action, there is no unique set of rules that we can be *said* to be 'following'.

Wittgenstein uses the term 'grammar' in two senses. In one of these, it is the enterprise of describing language-games. I have called this task 'Phenomenology of the Everyday'. In its other sense, it refers to the elements constituting these language-games: word-use, contexts of this use, and phenomena referred to by it.

Finally, a criterion for X is any phenomenon on the basis of which it makes sense to call something a case of X. For instance, a criterion for being in pain is pain-behaviour (in a situation where the lack of deception is evident), and a criterion for knowing how to ride a bike is doing so unaided. An important component of one's practical knowledge of words is knowledge of the criteria governing their use in descriptions of phenomena and ascriptions to entities. Hence a major portion of the task of Phenomenology of the Everyday is to uncover the criteria for these descriptive and ascriptive uses.

Unless one is familiar with the analytical philosophy of language that dominated the philosophical environment in which Wittgenstein lived at Cambridge in the thirties and forties, one is apt not to be struck by the novelty of the viewpoint on language that these technical terms present. Like Wittgenstein himself in the *Tractatus*, all analytical philosophers before Wittgenstein – and still many after him – saw language as a special medium which perhaps, in virtue of its logical properties, possessed an intimate relation to the structure of the world. When considering language philosophically, they examined its logical features and did not think about whether the fact that language is a social form of interaction might undermine their considerations.

Wittgenstein's technical terms emphasize that the use of language, its public context, and the public phenomena this use refers to form a unity. This suggests that the understanding and description of language cannot be separated from the understanding and description of the disparate activities and contexts in which it is used. Hence these terms recommend that in doing philosophy one should view language as a phenomenon of ongoing social interaction. When the philosopher realizes that language is essentially a form of social behaviour he begins to think about philosophical problems about language in terms of its social nature. As a result, for example, if he wants to analyse concepts, he becomes more receptive to Wittgenstein's proposal about how to do so. And, most importantly, because it is clear that social phenomena in general lack logical properties, he begins to see that language possesses fewer such rigid attributes than he had previously thought.

As I said, these terms not only make Wittgenstein's method plausible, but they also actively guide someone following it. This does not mean that these terms are used in the description of phenomena; they are never so used. Rather 'guides' means that when it comes time to investigate a particular concept, say the concept of knowledge, one asks oneself questions such as the following: What is the language-game played with the word 'knowledge'?, What are the rules governing its use?, What is the grammar of the word?, and What are the criteria for its use? Asking these questions directs one's attention to the phenomena called cases of knowledge and the contexts surrounding the use of this word. Hence they direct one to the phenomena, the examination of which elucidates the concept of knowledge and reveals what knowledge is.

The interpretative sciences of man

In the 'Remarks on Frazer's *Golden Bough*', one reads that the descriptive method and the type of understanding that Wittgenstein assigns to philosophy also apply to the interpretative sciences of man (*RFG* 35–5(241–2)). In order to achieve understanding in either history or social anthropology, Wittgenstein writes, all one needs to do is 'arrange the factual material so that we can easily pass from one part to another and have a clear view of it – showing it in a 'perspicuous' (*übersichtlichen*) way' (*RFG* 35(241)). The factual material is gathered by description of historical facts or of aspects of a foreign peoples' practices. Hence this method is formally identical to the philosophical method that perspicuously arranges descriptions of cases of X. Further: 'This perspicuous presentation makes possible that understanding that consists just in the fact that we "see the connection (*Zusammenhänge*)" ' (*RFG* 35(241)). Just as in philosophy one seeks to understand how the cases of X 'hang together', in the interpretative sciences of man one seeks to understand how the known elements of a human activity fit together as a coherent whole. I say 'interpretative sciences of man' and not 'social anthropology and history' alone, because first, there are related remarks about Freudian psychoanalysis in 'Conversations on Freud', and second, because a plausible way of making sense of the above pronouncements involves theses the truth of which has implications for any enterprise that attempts to understand human activities and practices.

I explained earlier that Wittgenstein believes that the description of phenomena, by preventing the philosopher from raising the philosophical problems that perplex him, allows the philosopher to be at peace with his work. Similarly, Wittgenstein suggests that only the description of historical and social phenomena can bring peace to the historian and anthropologist (*RFG* 30(236)). Imagine a historian confronted with a large amount of information about Rome at the time of Christ and suppose that her goal is to understand the changes Rome underwent during this era. According to Wittgenstein, there are two ways in which she can utilize this information in attempting to achieve this goal (compare what follows to *LC* 46). The first is to use it as a base for a hypothesis about the development that occurred in Rome at that time. Such a hypothesis goes beyond the collected data and speculates about events and factors about which there is as yet no information. Confirmation of this hypothesis requires additional information, and because of the relative unavailability of further historical data about Rome, if confirmation is at all possible, it will undoubtedly require an appreciable amount of time. Hence this method brings no peace to the historian. A second way of using this material is to 'see the data in their relations to one another and make a summary of them in a general picture' (*RFG* 34(241)). If the historian can construct such a general picture, then she achieves understanding and feels no need to continue investigating. If more information is uncovered, this picture can evolve and a new understanding be achieved. So she remains at peace with her work. But what makes this second approach an appropriate way of utilizing historical data and the understanding it achieves appropriate for historical phenomena? What is the goal of the interpretative sciences of man and what is it about human action and practices that makes this method and understanding applicable to them?

To begin to answer this, I will describe, in as common sense a way as possible, how Wittgenstein views the type of understanding sought by these sciences. In general, the goal of such sciences is to understand actions and practices. This understanding consists in understanding both why the actions occur and what people are doing in performing them. When confronted with a past historical event or an unfamiliar foreign practice, these things are not always apparent. One might know, say, that Caesar gave such and such an order but not understand why he does this nor what he is doing in issuing it. In general, one acquires an understanding of actions by placing them in a wider context of situation and culture. So by learning, for example, more about Caesar's goals, the possibilities of action open to him, and the habits of rulers living at his time to resort to a certain type of action for propaganda and intimidation effects, one learns what Caesar is up to. In fact, given these goals, possibilities, and habits, Caesar's action appears completely natural. Notice how such descriptions of context, without the use of a hypothetical explanation, tell one why actions occur. Wittgenstein suggests at *LC* 43–4 that one way of telling that one has achieved a proper understanding of an initially unintelligible action is when it is no longer necessary to search for a hypothetical explanation in order to make it intelligible. So the goal of the interpretative sciences of man is to make at first imperfectly understood activities appear completely natural, by describing enough of their contexts so that they seem perfectly sensible to us. (Wittgenstein makes similar comments about dream interpretation and dream symbols at *LC* 44–6.) I will explain later why description of context makes actions intelligible.

Success in making a social phenomenon intelligible by just describing its context requires that the investigator and the people whose actions he tries to understand be similar in certain ways. In exactly what ways they (and their situations) must be similar is a matter of some dispute, and it is not my concern to discuss this. Nevertheless, a word should be said about this problem so as to give the reader a feeling for its dimensions. Wittgenstein suggests (mostly in his remarks on Frazer) that this similarity consists in, at least, the following elements: a) common basic needs and emotions, b) similar physical environs (phases of the moon and seasons, animal and plant life), c) common facts of life (birth, death, sex), d) similar gestures and primitive reactions, e) shared beliefs, f) overt similarities in practices, g) environmental objects having the same significance (lions and thunder as threatening, caves and mothers as secure), and h) common goals and interests. Similarity along these lines provides a common ground to the anthropologist and his subjects. Because of it, for instance, aspects of the peoples' activities 'impress' the anthropologist 'as having meaning' (*LC* 42), and he is able to interpret actions as signs of emotions, attitudes, and desires with which he is familiar in his own culture. Hence this common ground permits the anthropologist initially to communicate with his subjects. It is subsequently built upon and supports the eventual achievement of an ability to understand them on a more or less everyday level. Such a common ground also plays an important role in making possible the understanding of historical events.

The type of understanding sought in the interpretative sciences of man is the very same type of everyday understanding one has of friends and other people living in one's culture. This understanding is unthematized except on the occasions when something puzzling or unintelligible occurs and the need arises explicitly to achieve it. One does this by filling out the context of the puzzling event. For instance, in response to the question, Why did John bring his galoshes to work?, nothing more is needed, in order to make this action intelligible, than the response: 'It looked threatening over Richmond.' Here an action which at first does not make sense, is rendered sensible by a description of its context. Similarly, as I just explained, it is the description of the context of a foreign or historical phenomenon that makes it seem sensible. And in neither case is it necessary to refer to anything hypothetical. So the goal of interpretative social science is explicitly to extend, to foreign peoples and past times, the largely unthematized understanding one possesses of one's fellows.

At this point, some of the parallels between interpretative science and philosophy are clear. In Wittgenstein's view, both utilize a method that consists in describing concrete situations – contexts of practices/events in one case, and contexts of word use and instances of concepts in the other. By skilfully arranging such descriptions, one acquires a clear view of them, an understanding of how they fit together. In the case of philosophy, as one progresses through a series of examples, one grasps the connections between cases of X and thus gradually comes to understand the concept of X. In the case of interpretative science, when one sees how various aspects of a practice fit together with the culture and other activities in which it is embedded, the practice begins to make sense and appear natural. And in both cases, there is no guarantee that this understanding can be verbally formulated. It might manifest itself simply in one's no longer feeling puzzled about what X is or what they are doing and why they are doing it. One the other hand, there is also no reason, at least in the case of interpretative science, to assume that no verbal formulation is possible.[7]

Action and society

I have by now left several loose threads dangling. These include: saying something more about why the description of the use of words elucidates concepts, explaining why the description of context makes action intelligible, and explaining why it is so easy to misunderstand language. To provide the needed explications, I will make use of two theses which I call 'The Thesis of Unreflective Action' and 'The Thesis of the Social Determination of Meaning and Understanding'. With their help it is possible both to complete my account and rationalize Wittgenstein's technical terms. It is important to realize that Wittgenstein nowhere explicitly discusses either of these theses. There is direct evidence for them in his work, but an equally important reason for attributing them to his philosophical vision is their ability to explain the above important features of his work.

The thesis of unreflective action claims that moment to moment human existence consists primarily in unreflective action – action neither directed nor observed by consciousness. The explanatory (and ontological) importance of consciousness was a significant element in philosophy from Descartes in the seventeenth century to

Husserl and the Logical Positivists in this century. This tradition assumed that it was always in and through consciousness – the region of reflective awareness – that a person controls his behaviour and takes cognizance of his surroundings. Wittgenstein rejects the notion that human beings, their activities, and culture are to be understood by reference to consciousness. He does this, in part, because he thinks that action is, on the whole, an unreflective reaction to the meaningfulness of the situation in which one is engrossed.

The idea behind this thesis is that human existence consists in a constant stream of reaction which is rarely, and only momentarily, held up by acts of conscious reflection about action. Action can, and does on the whole, proceed without conscious deliberation about *how* to act. For instance, in most goal-oriented action, one acts so as to achieve goals without consciously thinking, while acting, about how to do so; one's attention is not occupied with thinking, but is instead directed outwards to one's current situation. This is not to deny that we do sometimes consciously reflect about how to act; rather, the thesis points out how little of our daily lives is spent doing this.

Furthermore, action is not, in general, scrutinized by consciousness. Wittgenstein writes: 'When one means something, it is oneself meaning. So one is oneself in motion. One is rushing ahead and so cannot observe oneself rushing ahead. Indeed not' (*PI* 456). The words 'rushing ahead' are perfect. One is always 'on the go', doing one thing after another, all the while paying attention to the meaningful things in one's environment and not to what one is doing. Only occasionally does one hold up this flow of action by looking around one and taking stock of one's situation and behaviour.[8]

That Wittgenstein thought of human behaviour in this way is revealed by the remarks which point out that between being in a certain situation and acting in a certain way, no intermediate step need intervene. For instance, between being ordered to do X and obeying the order, no intermediate conscious event of any kind need occur (*Z* 283–9). Likewise, before applying colour words in common to a set of objects, there is no need to become aware of what the objects have in common (*BB* 130–36); rather, one sees the objects before one and without consciously recognizing, cognizing, or reflecting upon their all being red, one just says: 'They're (all) red' (cf. *Z* 136).

Not only is most daily adult action unreflective, but the entire edifice of language-games is based on unreflective action. Children do not ratiocinate when learning to speak. Rather, in virtue of being the kind of organisms they are (cf. *Z* 355) they interact with their environment and 'pick up' language before they are able to reflect. In doing so, they acquire the ability to speak without reflection as the situation warrants or demands. They learn forms of unreflective behaviour, ways of 'spontaneously' responding with words. Wittgenstein summarizes this state of affairs by writing: 'A language-game doesn't have its origin in reflection. Reflection is part of the language-game' (*Z* 391; Anscombe translation slightly altered).

The other thesis that I will utilize is the thesis that meaning and understanding are socially determined. For centuries, philosophers assumed that meaning, understanding, and language were either phenomena of consciousness or to be explained by reference to it. In the analytical tradition it was Wittgenstein who destroyed this conception. Where, for instance, Frege, the father of analytical philosophy, thought of meaning as that aspect of a word grasped by the mind, Wittgenstein claimed that the meaning of a word was its use. While many analytical philosophers conceived of understanding as an act of the mind, what it did when it grasped meaning, Wittgenstein maintained that understanding something was being able to do it, use it, or react coherently to it. (And I have already mentioned that analytical philosophers did not adequately think about how the social interactive nature of language is relevant to their concerns.)

Signs, Wittgenstein writes, are dead by themselves – their life is their use (*PI* 432). The slogan, 'the meaning of a word is its use', means simply that the meaning of a word is the role the word plays in linguistic actions (utterances and acts of writing). Wittgenstein thinks, however, that it makes good sense to say that not only linguistic expressions, but a wide variety of items have meaning ('The characteristic feature of the awakening human spirit is that a phenomenon has meaning for it' (*RFG* 33(239)); he discusses, for instance, gestures, musical notes, blueprints, and parts of picture puzzles (*Z* 170, 201, 157–75, 219). Anything that can play a role in our activities has meaning, and the determinants of meaning are whatever determines the roles that these linguistic and non-linguistic items play. Wittgenstein mentions: custom, the way people are brought up, culture, activities, people's interests, past experiences, natural reactions, familiarity with language, and above all, the circumstances surrounding the phenomenon that possesses meaning (cf., for example, *PI* p. 201; *Z* 164–5, 170). As this list suggests, the determinants of meaning are primarily social (though nothing precludes biological factors from having an influence here). This has the consequence that if one wants to understand the meaning of some item, one must uncover the (largely social) factors determinative of its role in our activities.

Understanding, for Wittgenstein, is neither an inner event of 'getting it' (he does not deny that such events occur, only that understanding always consists in them), nor a state of a person, as of a hypothetical mechanism, that enables one to do what one does. Rather it is being able to participate in the activities and language-games of the form of life into which one has been trained (cf. *PI* 143–55; *Z* 157–75). For instance, understanding the rule governing a sequence of numbers is being able to continue the sequence (citing the rule is not enough, because one can cite a rule without being able to operate with it). Likewise, understanding the meaning of a sentence is being able, for instance, to explain this meaning to others, or being able to use the sentence in ways intelligible to others. Understanding X is a 'being-able': a being able to use X, say something about it, or take up a meaningful stance towards it (cf., for example, *PI* 636). And one shows one's understanding by using it, talking about it, or taking up the stance.

People acquire understanding by being trained into a form of life. Hence, it is predominantly social factors that determine understanding. In fact, the factors that determine meaning are the factors that determine understanding. So the meanings of phenomena and one's understanding of them are complementary: by being socialized, one comes to understand the roles items play in our activities, and correlatively, an item plays no role that is not understood by someone.

With these theses, it is now possible to tie up the loose ends that I mentioned earlier. The idea that action is unreflective makes it clear why philosophers are so prone to misunderstand language: speaking a language involves knowing how to react with words in ways relevant to one's situation, but it does not involve a reflective grasp of what goes on when one so acts. So while it is easy to speak, it is not easy to command a clear view of the language-game played with any particular word. 'We talk, we utter words, and only later get a picture of their life' (*PI* p. 209). Not having consciously observed how we talk, these pictures are usually incorrect.

It is the thesis that meaning and understanding are socially determined that casts additional light on why the examination of the use of language elucidates concepts. According to this thesis, in order to understand the use (meaning) of a word, one must uncover the factors determining it. These factors together form the context of this use. Hence, in order to uncover the grounds for this use, more particularly, the grounds of the way it classifies phenomena, one must look at its context. Thus to understand the concept expressed by the word, one must describe the contexts of the use of the word and phenomena called cases of the concept expressed by it. Furthermore, as I said, the factors that determine the use of a word are the factors that determine one's (practical) understanding of this use. So in describing this use, one simultaneously reveals this understanding. This is why it is possible to characterize Wittgenstein's method as an attempt to render practical understanding explicit.

As for Wittgenstein's technical terms, these terms, as I discussed earlier, both express the embeddedness of language within social activities and bring this to the attention of the philosopher who investigates language. Given the theses of unreflective action and the social determination of meaning and understanding, it is clear why Wittgenstein would choose to use them. The theses also further explicate his ideas about rules.

There was one prominent philosophical way of thinking about 'rule-governed' behaviour that maintained that rules make people do what they do. One reason offered in favour of this idea was that in order to be said to be following a rule, one must apply it or interpret it at each step of the proceedings in order to know what to do. Against this, the idea that action is unreflective argues that between being in a situation and acting, no conscious step need intervene. So actions in accordance with rules cannot, in general, issue from conscious applications of those rules.

More generally, it is Wittgenstein's view that social factors impose regularities upon actions. Hence insofar as individual speech acts and acts of writing are parts of regularities in linguistic action, it is social forces, of which (explicit) rules form only a small part, that determine what we do. Thus Wittgenstein reinterprets the notion of rule involved in the idea that practices are rule-governed, so that it is no longer the idea of something which guides action by being involved in it, but is a way of describing regularities in unreflective action determined by social factors. Note how unreflective action and socially determined semantics support each other: it is the effectiveness of social factors and not conscious guiding of one's action that enables people to act in ways intelligible to each other.

Turning now to the interpretative sciences of man, it will be useful if I sketch the general picture of action that emerges when one relates the two theses that I have been discussing: People act because of and according to the way in which phenomena about them present themselves as meaningful, and phenomena acquire meaning in virtue of social factors which give them actual and possible roles in our activities. So why is it that description of the contexts of actions and practices renders them intelligible?

According to the thesis of unreflective action, in order to make a primitive ritual or historical event intelligible, one must ascertain how the situation in which the actors find themselves is meaningful to them. In other words, one must extend one's everyday understanding of one's social colleagues to embrace the understanding that the performers of as yet unintelligible actions have of their situation. The thesis that meaning and understanding are socially determined stipulates that the factors that determine their understanding lie in the social context of their activities; so, too, do the items that they understand. Hence one will grasp their understanding by describing this context. By learning, for example, the role the ritual plays in their life, the roles that artifacts and symbols used in it play in a wider context of activities, how children are introduced to it, the story people tell about it, and so on, one uncovers how the people understand their situation. Thereby their actions become intelligible.

Something related occurs when John's bringing his galoshes to work is made intelligible by a description of the weather. This description tells the person who asks about John's action what it was in John's situation to which John responded. Here, because the questioner and John share the understanding that threatening sky over Richmond means 'protect oneself from rain', indicating that it was to a threatening sky that John responded is sufficient to make his action intelligible. Unlike the case of the anthropologist who, confronted with the ritual, needs to discover the meaning of the phenomena to which the people respond, there is no need to investigate further the meaning of the threatening sky. (If John had worn *Lederhosen* instead of galoshes that day, a description of the weather would not, by itself, make his action intelligible, even if it *was* the weather that induced his behaviour. One would still need to know the (peculiar) meaning the weather has for John.)

Theories and the study of human activity

At this point I can say something more about Wittgenstein's hostility to the use of theories in the interpretative sciences of man. As I discussed, according to Wittgenstein, these sciences proceed by describing, in everyday terms, both the items that people understand and the factors determining their understanding. There are two reasons why this description must be in everyday terms. The first is that because what one wants to capture is the (everyday) way people understand their situation, one must describe this situation in the everyday, ordinary way that people understand it. The second reason is that what one is trying to extend is one's own everyday understanding, and this is possible only by using descriptions of the type used in everyday life. Theories, however, abandon the level of everyday description, and describe social phenomena as variations on particular archetypes or as combinations of theoretical parameters. They thus must renounce any claim to achieve the type of understanding that is the goal of the interpretative sciences of man. For the purposes of *these* sciences, theory is, at best, useless, and at worst, obstructive.

More generally, recall that in discussing Wittgenstein's views on concepts, I explained how Wittgenstein thinks that the instances of a given concept form a far more heterogeneous group than recognized by philosophical theories. He makes a similar claim about human affairs in general. The factors that determine the shape and course of human activities are immense in number. Wittgenstein points out, for instance, that there is a variety of reasons and causes for why children play(*LC* 49) and a wide selection of causes for punishment (*LC* 50). It is typical of researchers in *all* the human sciences, however, to ignore the complex variety of factors that determine the characteristics of the objects of their study; and their theories give the impression that these factors are far less numerous than is actually the case. While discussing Freud's dream theory, for instance, Wittgenstein remarks that it suffers from attempting to provide one form of explanation for the entire manifold of dream phenomena (*LC* 43, 47–8). Likewise, he criticizes Frazer for offering a single form of explanation for all primitive magic rituals. One could say that, in Wittgenstein's view, these scientists, like philosophers, are in the grip of overly simple and misleading pictures.

So, in Wittgenstein's view, the problem with theories in the study of human affairs is that they always give explanations that do not take into account the entire range of factors that affect the phenomena they study. As a result, they never give an adequate account of their subject matter. The only way of capturing this range of factors, according to Wittgenstein, is via a descriptive technique of the type he introduces.[9] It is important to remember that this methodological claim holds only for those sciences that study human affairs. It does not apply to natural science, although it does pertain to so-called 'noninterpretative' human sciences such as economics.

Is it possible to give a theory whose parameters *are* sufficiently rich to capture this variety of factors? The answer to this question depends, of course, on just how complex human affairs are. If this complexity is not too great, then the possibility of such a theory depends on the skills of theoreticians. (Wittgenstein is undoubtedly correct, though, that the construction of such a theory must be preceded by description of the variety of factors affecting the phenomena one studies.) It is clear, however, that at the time that Wittgenstein wrote, no theory that even approximated this ideal had ever been proposed; and the situation is, arguably, the same today. This may be connected with the fact that one of the prime criteria for an acceptable theory is simplicity; the urge to theorize is, in part, an urge to simplify. So it is contrary to one of the desiderata of theory-building to construct a theory sufficiently complex to capture this range of factors.

Sometimes, however, it seems that Wittgenstein wants to claim that human affairs are so complex that no theory can *ever* be adequate to the facts. If he is right, then the only possible human science is interpretative (descriptive) human science. But I do not see any way of proving the matter one way or the other.

In any case, there are seeds of a new theory in Wittgenstein's own work. When one combines the thesis of unreflective action with the thesis of the social determination of meaning and understanding, there results a picture of human action according to which, as I described earlier, action is a response to the socially determined intelligibility of phenomena in one's current situation. Human activ-

iιy and culture at large is a self-perpetuating process in which individuals react to socially established constellations of intelligibility, in
so doing maintaining these constellations and sometimes establishing
new ones, which, in turn, form the context for new occasions of action
to which individuals respond – and so on. This picture is so general
that it seems that if it ·vas elaborated and filled in, it could capture a
great deal (but probaι y not all) of the complexity of human affairs. A
human science that, by combining theoretical reflection and everyday
description, attempted to do this, would have to determine, among
other things: the types of social factors that set up and enforce
constellations of intelligibility, how they accomplish this, what it is
about human beings such that they respond to such constellations,
and how everyday social existence is structured such that unreflective
action is possible.

Whether or not this is *just another* distorted and overly simple
picture, only time and effort can tell. In any case, it is incorrect to
assume that the task of concretizing it is a task for any one discipline –
it is an enterprise to which philosophers, biologists, literary critics,
and writers have as much to contribute as sociologists, psychologists,
social anthropologists, poets and historians. Thus the elaboration of
Wittgenstein's (and early Heidegger's) vision of the place of action in
society calls out for the collaboration of philosophy with the *Geisteswissenschaften*.[10] [11]

6

The Significance of Significance: the Case of Cognitive Psychology

Charles Taylor

The two approaches to philosophy which the editors in their introduction dub the 'Enlightenment' and the 'understanding' approaches are not only distinguished by a different attitude to natural science. They also constitute different schools of thought within the sciences of man, and carry on their rivalry within these. This is, perhaps, particularly noticeable in psychology, which has always been peculiarly close to philosophy, indeed, was born, in a sense, out of philosophy: the first theories of modern psychology were those propounded by philosophers of the modern 'ways of ideas'.

I want in this paper to map a bit of the front, in which the trench warfare between the two views is now being carried on. This segment is around a new position, often referred to by the term 'cognitive psychology', which is used to designate a range of theories which purport to explain intelligent human performances in terms of computations, on the model of those we are familiar with in present day digital computers.

These theories were born partly out of the remarkable achievements of computer science, and partly out of deep dissatisfaction with the more and more evident inadequacies of behaviourism to cope with skilled performances of all kinds. Philosophers who support this new approach[1] see themselves as having broken with the taboos of behaviourism. The computer paradigm enables them to embrace 'mentalistic' explanations without repudiating their allegiances to natural science or materialism.

The philosophical debate between the supporters of cognitive psychology and its critics[2] illustrates all the principal features of the battle between 'Enlightenment' and 'understanding' views. And most striking of all, when two such different approaches square off, the most difficult thing is to bring about a genuine confrontation. For as with all deep philosophical differences, what is at stake is the relevance of the arguments; since there is a disagreement even about what is at stake, what should count as an argument is in dispute. What each side sees as its best arguments tend to pass the interlocutors by, to seem beside the point.

As we shall see, even the historical identity of the parties is in dispute. Supporters of cognitive psychology see themselves as having broken decisively with the metaphysic of the age of positivism and behaviourism. In particular, they see their view as anti-reductionist. For their opponents, however, the continuities with the Enlightenment tradition are much more salient, and reductionism is still very much in evidence.

I want in what follows to try to trace the argument about cognitive psychology, identify the source of the cross-purposes, and bring the two views to a confrontation around what I see to be the crucial issue. The resulting map will, of course, be far from neutral. But is there such a thing as an account of a philosophical dispute which is both illuminating and neutral? That being said, I acknowledge the gnawing fear that mine may be neither.

I

Perhaps a good point of entry into the argument is the observation which naturally occurs to philosophers of the 'understanding' approach, particularly those with a background in phenomenology, when they contemplate the theories of cognitive psychology: that's not at all how we experience action. Crucial misunderstandings arise around the *point* of this observation.

To spell it out a little, we can take our everyday performances, like catching a ball, or carrying on a conversation. The current mainstream in cognitive psychology sees as its task to explain these by some underlying process which resembles a computation. When we reflect, we are struck by the skill we exhibit in these performances: knowing just where to reach to intercept the ball, knowing just where and how to stand, what tone to adopt, what nuance of phrasing to use, to respond appropriately to what our interlocutor has said. To explain the performance would then be to give an account of how we compute these responses, how we take in the data, process it, and work out what moves to make, given our goals.

To reach an answer by computation is to work it out in a series of explicit steps. The problem is defined, if necessary broken up into sub-problems, and then resolved by applying procedures which are justified by the definition. We resort to computation sometimes when we can't get the answer we want any other way; and sometimes when we want to show that this is the right answer. Explicit procedures can be crucial to a justification of our result.

But in the case of skilled performances like the above, we aren't aware of any computation. That's not what we're *doing*, in the sense of an activity that we're engaged in and could be got to avow and take responsibility for, granted undistorted self-knowledge. The computation would have to be an underlying process, on a par with – or indeed, identical with – the electrical discharges in brain and nervous system.

The nature of the activity as *we* carry it on is in some respects antithetical to a computation. When we catch the ball, or respond appropriately to our neighbour's conversational opening over the back fence, we make no explicit definition of the problem. Indeed, we would be very hard put to it to make one, even if we set ourselves the task, and might find it beyond our powers. There is correspondingly no break-down into sub-problems, or application of procedures. We operate here, as in most contexts, with the task implicit, that is, not expressly formulated. That's part of what people mean when they say that we're applying know-how here, not explicit knowledge.

Our awareness of our activity shows that computation is something we do sometimes, not all the time. But more, we can see that it is quite beyond our powers to do it all the time. It is not just that there are some performances where an explicit definition of the problem seems beyond our capacity. The fact also is that every activity of computation deploys skilled performances which are themselves not explicitly thematized, and can't be right now without disrupting the computation in train. As I define my problem in some explicit formulation, I draw on my capacity to use language, build declarative sentences, zero in on salient issues, and others again, which I have to leave tacit for the moment while concentrating on the matter at hand. In different ways, Wittgenstein and Polanyi have made us aware of this inescapable horizon of the implicit surrounding activity, which the latter discusses in terms of 'tacit knowing'.

On the other hand, it is clear that we can only match these performances on a machine by defining the problems explicitly and building the machine to compute. There is nothing comparable to our experience of tacit knowledge in a machine. The fact that we have in the last half century developed the theory of such machines, and then made considerable progress in building them, has been of great moment for psychology. It has given rise to a new explanatory paradigm, which seems to offer the hope of a materialistic theory of behaviour, which would not be as idiotically reductive as classical behaviourism.

It is the prestige of this paradigm – and the strength of the underlying commitment to a mechanistic materialism – which powers cognitive psychology; that, and the continuing influence of the epistemological tradition of rational reconstruction. We are after all material objects, susceptible like all others to some mechanistic explanation: so runs the reasoning. We are moreover material objects which bring off these extraordinary performances of ball catching and conversation. Where more plausible to look for an explanation than in that other range of things which we design to realize (supposedly) comparable performances, viz., computing machines?

The observation which might occur to phenomenologists, that cognitive psychology offers an account quite at variance with our experience of action, is set aside as irrelevant. After all, why should the features of the correct explanation be accessible to experience?

But is this really irrelevant? Or are the two sides at cross-purposes here? This is what I'd now like to explore. More generally, I want to ask whether features which are crucial to our self-understanding as agents can be accorded no place in our explanatory theory. Is this extrusion a justified move towards a properly scientific theory, or is it rather a way of side-stepping the important explanatory issues, of 'changing the subject', as Davidson puts it?

The implicit/explicit distinction is one such important feature. Before grappling with the main question, I'd like briefly to introduce another. This resides in the fact that human beings are self-interpreting animals. This means among other things that there is no adequate description of how it is with a human being in respect of his/her existence as a person which does not incorporate his/her self-understanding, i.e., the descriptions which he or she is inclined to give of his/her emotions, aspirations, desires, aversions, admiration, etc. What we are at any moment is, one might say, partly constituted by our self-understanding.

This is another feature unmatched by machines; or we find in them only the weakest analogies. A computer may indeed be monitoring some of its own operations, and this may seem an analogue to self-understanding. But, in this case, there is a clear distinction between description and object. The operations are there independent of the monitoring, even if this may bring about other operations which interact with them. But in our case, our self-understanding shapes how we feel, for example, in such a way that there isn't an answer to the question: what is our state of feeling? independent of our self-description. The analytical distinction description/object can't be made.

To look at some examples: I love A, I admire B, I am indignant at the behaviour of C. My love for A is, let's say, not just a momentary *élan*; it is bound up with the sense that our lives are permanently or definitively linked, that being with her is an essential part of being who I am. Now these last clauses constitute a description of how I feel. They are not just predictions or counterfactuals based on what I feel. I am not just predicting, e.g., that were we to separate, I should feel terrible, or be at a loss. What I am doing is describing the quality of my emotion, which is quite different in what it is and how it feels from other kinds of attachment which lack this defining character.

And the quality of the emotion is essentially given by this description; that is, having this emotion is defined in terms of being inclined to give this kind of description. This is not to say that there are not cases where one might love in this way and not be ready to describe one's feelings in this way. One might only later come to recognize that this sense of lives being joined was the essential character of one's feeling. But in attributing the feeling to oneself even before one was ready to speak in this way, one is still saying something about one's self-understanding. When I say that I loved her in this way last year, before I came to understand properly how our lives are bound up together, I am grounding myself on the sense I had then of her importance to me, and I am purporting to give a more adequate characterization of that sense. Presumably, I was even then making plans which involved a lifetime together, or committing myself to some long-term path, and it is in virtue of *that* that I can say now: 'I loved her in this way then'.

Put another way, I couldn't attribute this kind of love to an agent who was incapable of having in any form whatever the sense of being bound to someone for life. That's why we can't attribute many human emotions to animals. Some animals do in fact mate for life; but they can't have the kind of love we're talking about, because this requires the sense that it's for life, and therefore the possibility of making a distinction between the passing and the permanent.

Thus even before we are fully conscious of it, this emotion is characterized essentially by our self-understanding, by the sense we have of the meaning of its object to us. Similar points could be made in relation to admiration and indignation. We admire someone whom we think is great, or exceptional, or exhibits some virtue to a high degree. This emotion is defined by this kind of understanding of its object. And once again, this doesn't prevent us ascribing admiration to people who don't recognize their favourable judgements of those they admire. I recognize now that I not only felt well-disposed towards B, but I also admired him. I didn't want to admit it at the time, because I have trouble avowing that I grudgingly recognize a virtue in his way of being. But I acknowledge that I have all along, and *therefore* that I admired him then, albeit without recognizing it. I can only attribute the admiration retrospectively because I attribute the virtue-judgement retrospectively as well. I see it there, in the things I thought and said and did, even though I didn't allow it its right name. A parallel point could be made about the judgement encapsulated in indignation, that the object of our feeling has done some flagrant wrong.

In this way our feelings are constituted by our self-understandings; so that, as I said above, the properly human feelings can't be attributed to animals; and some feelings are specific to certain cultures. But all this in a way which defeats any attempt to distinguish description and object. If one searches for some core of feeling which might exist independently of the sense of its object which constitutes it, one searches in vain. More, the very nature of human emotion has eluded one. An emotion is essentially constituted by our sense of its object, i.e., by what we are inclined to say about its significance for us. That's what is contained in the slogan that human beings are self-interpreting animals: there is no such thing as what they are, independently of how they understand themselves. To use Bert Dreyfus's evocative phrase, they are interpretation all the way down.

This is a second feature of ourselves, as we understand our activity and feeling, which has no machine analogue. And in fact the two features are linked.

I was arguing above that we can have a certain emotion before we are ready to apply what we can later recognize as the essential description. We can make these later attributions in virtue of what descriptions we were ready to make, which we retrospectively understand as expressing the sense of things which is properly encapsulated in the essential description. Our emotions can be better or less well understood by ourselves, can be more or less explicitly formulated. We might want to say: 'yes, I loved her in this way before, but it wasn't explicitly formulated for me as it is now; it was still something implicit, unsaid, unrecognized'.

But this transposition from the implicit to the explicit is an important one. The emotion itself changes. An emotion clarified is in some way an emotion transformed. This is a corollary of the fact that emotions are constituted by self-understandings. And it will typically play an important part in our explaining someone's behaviour that he didn't explicitly understand what he was feeling, or perhaps that at the crucial moment he began to understand explicitly.

In other words, because of our nature as self-interpreting animals, the quality of our self-understanding plays an important role, and the distinction implicit/explicit has a crucial explanatory relevance; that is, it has relevance in the understanding we have of ourselves as agents and subjects of feeling.

Now there is no analogue of this in computing machines. The connected features of self-interpretation and a partly implicit sense of things have no place there. Should this worry us in adopting such machines as paradigms for the explanation of human performance?

II

No, say the cognitivists, why should this worry us? It wouldn't be the first time that the way things look to the uninstructed eye, or to ordinary consciousness, or to commonsense, turns out to be misleading. The progress of science is littered with such overrulings of appearance. Right back at the beginning, we had to disregard the fact that the sun seems to go around the earth, that moving objects feel as though they stop when we cease to exert effort. Now we recognize that the four-dimensional space-time continuum of ordinary awareness is crucially different from the one invoked in physics. Closer to home, we learn that the pain in my arm really comes from a malfunction of the heart; that the pain I feel in the area of the heart in my hypochondriac panic really comes from my pectoral muscles. Why should the case be any different with acting, thinking, feeling?

The answer to this (would-be rhetorical) question might be that the supposedly phenomenal features of action and understanding are an essential part of the explanation.

An objection that comes to mind straight off to the proposal that we explain human skilled performance in terms of underlying processes resembling those of computing machines is this: the two kinds of process differ in what looks like a crucial respect.

We do attribute some of the same terms to both humans and machines. We speak of both as 'calculating', or 'deducing', and so on for a long list of mental performance terms. But the attribution doesn't carry the same force in the two cases, because we cannot really attribute action to a machine in the full-blooded sense.

Why do we want to say that a machine computes, or for that matter that a machine moves gravel, or stacks bottles? Partly because the machine operates in such a way as to get these tasks done in the proper circumstances. But also, and more strongly, in the case, e.g., of computers, because the way the machine gets these tasks done has a certain structural resemblance to the way we do them. Characteristically, the machine's operation involves breaking down the task into sub-tasks, the fulfilment of which can be seen as logical stages to the completion of the computation; and this breaking down into sub-tasks is essential to what we call computation when *we* compute – you wouldn't say someone was computing, if he gave the answer straight off without any analytical reflection.

More generally, to borrow Fodor's formulation, we can see a physical system as a computational device, if we can map different physical stages of that system onto formulae of some language of computation, in such a way that the causal relations between the physical states match the logical relations among the formulae. 'The idea is that, in the case of organisms as in the case of real computers, if we get the right way of assigning formulae to the states it will be feasible to interpret the sequence of events that causes the output as a computational derivation of the output.'[3]

Thirdly, we say that a machine 'does' something when we have designed it to accomplish the task. All three factors apply in the case of computers; at least two in the case of bottle-stackers. But there could be objects which we would describe as *phi-ing* just because they were very useful at accomplishing the task of getting something *phi-ed*, even though they were discovered in nature and not manufactured.

But it is clear from this that the attribution of an action-term to such artifacts or useful objects is relative to our interests and projects. A machine *phi-s* because we have manufactured it to *phi*, or we use it to *phi*, or we are interested in it in respect of the *phi-ing* it gets done. If we ask why we want to say that it is *phi-ing* and not *psi-ing*, where 'things being *psi-ed*' is a description of some other outcome of the machine's operation (our computer also hums, heats up the room, keeps George awake, increases our electricity bill), the answer is that *psi-ing* is not what we use it for, or what we built it for.

Of course, we normally would say quite unproblematically that the machine hums, heats the room, etc.; but where we want to make a distinction between what it's really engaged in, as against just incidentally bringing about (it's a computer, dammit, not a room-heater), we do so by reference to our interests, projects, or designs. A changed economic picture, or the demands of a new technology, could make it the case the *psi-ing* was suddenly a very important function, and then we might think of the same machine as a *psi-er* and as *psi-ing* (provided it also was an efficient device for this end). Indeed, we could imagine two groups, with quite different demands, sharing time on the same device for quite different purposes. The computer also makes clicks in strange patterns, very much valued by some eccentric group of meditation adepts. For them, the machine is a 'mantric clicker', while for us it is computing payrolls, or *chi* squares.

But what is it *really* doing? There is no answer to the question for a machine. We tend to think in this case that it is really computing, because we see it as made for this purpose, and only by accident serving the purpose of helping meditation. But this is a contingent, external fact, one external, that is, to the machine's make-up and function. It could have been designed by some mad yogi with a degree in electronic engineering, and just happen to serve as a computer. Or it could just have come into existence by some cosmic accident: a bolt of many-tongued lightning fused all this metal into just the structure needed to fulfil both these functions.

So attributions of action-terms to such devices are relative to our interests and purposes. As Fodor puts it: 'It is *feasible* to think of such a system as a computer just insofar as it is possible to devise some mapping which pairs physical states of the device with formulae in a computing language in such a fashion as to preserve the desired semantic relations among the formulae.'[4] And he adds later: 'Patently, there are indefinitely many ways of pairing states of the machine with formulae in a language which will preserve the right sort of relation.'

But the same is not true of ourselves. There is an answer to the question, what is he doing? or what am I doing? – when it is not taken in the bland form such that any true description of an outcome eventuating in the course of my action can provide an answer – which is not simply relative to the interests and purposes of the observer. For action is directed activity. An action is such that a certain outcome is privileged, that which the agent is seeking to encompass in the action.

This purpose may be unconscious, as when my awareness of certain desires is repressed; it may be partly unformulated, as when I walk in such a way as to avoid the holes in the pavement while concentrating on something else; it may be at the margins of attention, as when I doodle while talking on the phone. But in all these cases, our willingness to talk about action depends on our seeing the activity as directed by the agent, on their being such a privileged outcome, which the agent is trying to encompass. This is the basis of the distinction between action and non-action (e.g. events in inanimate objects, or reflex-type events in ourselves, or lapses, breakdowns, etc.).

So in contradistinction to machines, we attribute action to ourselves in a strong sense, a sense in which there is an answer to the question, what is he doing? which is not merely relative to the interests and purposes of an observer. Of course, there are issues between different action descriptions which may be settled by the interests of the observer. For any action may bear a number of descriptions. Notoriously, there are further and more immediate purposes, broader and narrower contexts of relevance. So we can say severely, 'I know you just wanted to do the best by him, but did you physically prevent him leaving the house?', or 'I know you only meant to scare him, but did you shoot the dog?'. Here we have classic examples of the distinction between the description which is salient for the agent, and that which is crucial for someone assessing his conduct.

But however great the interest-relative variability in the description of what I do, a distinction can be drawn among the outcomes that eventuate in my action between what I do under whatever description, and the things that cannot be attributed to me at all in any full-blooded sense. This distinction is not observer-, or user-, or designer-relative; and that is the difference with machines.

Thus there are descriptions of things which get done when I act which I can repudiate as action descriptions: e.g., that I move molecules of air when I talk, or even give clicks with my teeth which are highly prized by the eccentric meditation circle. We can imagine that they hire me to come and give lectures in philosophy, and I am puzzled when they keep inviting me back, because they don't seem interested in what I say, and indeed, sink into a deep trance when I talk. There is some sense in which 'putting them to sleep' is an action description applying to me; but we recognize that this applies in a quite different way than, e.g., the description 'lecturing on philosophy'; and hence we have a barrage of reservation terms, like 'unwittingly', 'inadvertently', 'by accident', 'by mistake', and so on.

Now *this* distinction, between what I am full-bloodedly doing, and what is coming about inadvertently, etc., is not relative to observer's or designer's interests and purposes. Unlike the case of the artifact, it remains true of me that what I'm doing in the full-blooded sense is lecturing on philosophy, and not mantric clicking; even though everyone else becomes interested in mantric clicking, and no-one even knows what philosophy is any more besides me.

Nor can we account for this difference by casting me in the role of crucial observer, and saying that the crucial description is the one relative to my interests. For this neglects the vital difference, that with the artifact the observer's interests are distinguishable from the machine. So that it makes sense to speak of a machine as surviving with its functioning intact even when no-one is interested any more in its original purpose, and it serves quite another one, or none at all. But an action is essentially constituted by its purpose. This is a corollary of the point above, that men are self-interpreting animals. The attempt to make a comparable distinction to the one we make with artifacts, between external movement and some separable inner act of will, breaks down, as is now notorious; for the inner act shrinks to vanishing point. Our ordinary conception of an act of will is parasitic on our ordinary understanding of action.

So mental performance terms, like 'calculating' have a different sense when attributed to artifacts than when attributed to humans. In the latter case, we mean to describe actions in the strong sense, in a way which is not merely observer- or user- or designer-relative. Let me say quickly, as a sort of parenthesis, that this represents as yet no decisive objection against cognitivism; it just puts the issue about it in clearer perspective. It is a point about the logic of our action-attributions. It doesn't show by itself that what goes on when people calculate is something very different than what goes on in computers. For all we can say at this stage, a computer-type, observer-relative 'calculation' may underly every act of calculating; and it may provide the best explanation for our performance.

The point is only that our language of action attributes something quite different to us agents, viz., action in the strong sense; something for which there is no basis whatever in machines, or in the functioning of the organism understood analogously to that of a machine; and indeed, for which one cannot easily conceive of any basis being found in a machine.

I have made the point in terms of action, but the same point goes for other 'functional' states of machines in contrast to ourselves. We might try to find states of machines which parallel our desires and emotions. A machine might be said to 'want to go' when it is all primed, and started, and only being held back by a brake, say. But it is clear that an analogous distinction applies here to the one in the case of action. What the machine 'desires' is determined by the observer's interest or fiat, or that of the user or designer; while this is not so for the human agent. Actually, the temptation doesn't even exist here, as it does in the case of action, to apply such terms to machines, except as a kind of anthropomorphic joke.

This is because the crucial difference is even more evident here than in the case of action. For the clear upshot of the above discussion is that human and animal agents are beings for whom the question arises of what significance things have for them. I am using the term 'significance' here as a general term of art to designate what provides our non-observer-relative answers to such questions as, what is he doing? what is she feeling? what do they want? etc.

Ascribing action in the strong sense to some being is treating that being as a subject of significance. The full-blooded action description gives us the action as purposed by the agent. We define the action by the significance it had for the agent (albeit sometimes unconsciously), and this is not just one of many descriptions from different observers' standpoints, but is intrinsic to the action *qua* action. So we can only attribute action to beings we see as subjects of significance, beings for whom things can have significance in a non-observer-relative way.

We have to add this last rider, because there is, of course, another, weaker sense in which we can speak of things having significance for inanimate beings: something can be dangerous for my car, or good for my typewriter. But these significances are only predicable in the light of extrinsic, observer-relative or user-relative purposes. By contrast, the significances we attribute to agents in our language of action and desire are their own. It is just the principal feature of agents that we can speak about the meanings things have for them in this non-relative way, that, in other words, things *matter* for them.

Let's call this essential feature of agents the 'significance feature'. Then the crucial difference between men and machines is that the former have it while the latter lack it.

This difference is less immediately evident to us in wielding our action-descriptions, or at least some of them. For action-descriptions focus our attention on what gets done; that action is directed by the agent is usually subsidiary to our main point of concern. Thus we have no trouble applying action terms in a weaker sense to inanimate things. But desire- or feeling-descriptions focus our attention directly on the significance things have for the agent. That's why there is something strained or metaphoric in applying these to machines.

The strain gets even greater when we come to emotion terms. We might speak of our car as 'raring to go', because at least 'going' is something it is capable of, albeit in a weak, user-relative sense. But when we get to an emotion term like 'shame', we couldn't have even the remotest temptation to apply it to the inanimate.

'Shame' is in fact intrinsically bound up with the significance feature. One might say, doubly bound up. It is not just that to attribute shame is to say that the situation has a certain significance for the agent: it is humiliating, or reflects badly on him, or something of the kind. It is also that the significance or import of the situation is one which only makes sense in relation to beings with the significance feature.

This contrasts with an import like danger, for instance. My car can be in danger, if there is a rock about to fall on it, for instance. This is, of course, a user-relative attribution: the danger is only to it in its function as car; *qua* collection of metal and glass bits, the rock represents no danger. But at least the attribution user-relatively makes sense. A car *qua* car can be in danger.

But 'shame' points to a different kind of import. Someone can only experience shame who has a sense of himself as an agent. For I feel ashamed of what I am like/how I appear as an *agent* among other agents, a subject of significance among others. It may seem sometimes that the immediate object of my shame is some physical property that a non-agent could bear. I may be ashamed of my small stature, or outsize hands. But these can only be objects of shame because of their significance: small stature means being overshadowed, failing to have a commanding presence among others; outsize hands embody indelicacy, lack of refinement, they are proper to peasants.

The import of danger can be physical destruction, and this can happen to a car *qua* car. But the import of shame touches us essentially as subjects of significance. It makes no sense to apply it to any but agents (and not even to all of them, not to animals for instance).

The significance feature is crucially bound up in our characterization of ourselves as agents. It underlies our attributing action to ourselves in a strong sense, as well as our attributions of desire and feeling; and reference to it is essentially involved in the definition of our emotions. With these, it is not just a matter of our attributing them to ourselves in a stronger sense than to inanimate objects; these concepts cannot get a grip on non-agents, even in a metaphorical manner. They only make sense in relation to us. In a world without self-aware agents, they could have no senseful application whatever.

The significance feature underlies the two features I singled out in the first section. We have these two, interpretation and the implicit/explicit distinction, because we are agents with a linguistic capacity, a capacity to formulate the significance things have for us.

But to formulate the significance of something, to make it explicit, is to alter it, as we saw above. This is because we are dealing with agents, subjects of non-observer-relative significance. My making explicit the danger my car is in doesn't alter the import of the situation for it; but my coming to see clearly the import of my situation for me can be *ipso facto* to alter its significance for me. Our being agents is a condition of our self-interpretations being constitutive of what we are; and it is because these interpretations can be explicitly formulated that the distinction implicit/explicit plays a crucial role for us.

These three features are closely connected, and are essential to us in our understanding of ourselves as agents.

III

Let's return to the main issue. Should the fact that our ordinary self-understanding attributes to us features which have no place in the computing machine paradigm make us wary of this in explaining human performances? Or can we dismiss these features as misleading surface appearance, on all fours with the sun's apparent movement around the earth?

At least a *prima facie* objection arises to just dismissing them. Aren't they an essential part of what we have to explain? This objection could be spelled out in the following way. We are asked to believe that some behaviour of ours in computing, or some behaviour which involves no computing but involves skilled selection of response, is to be explained on the same principles as those accounting for the operation of a computing machine. This is pressed as an overwhelmingly plausible line of approach, given the similarity in outcome given the (physically defined) input. (This claim involves a big promissory note, because there are all sorts of performances by us we haven't even begun to match on machines, but I won't take this up here.)[5] It appears plausible, in other words, because we seem to be able to apply terms like 'computing', 'figuring out the answer', 'finding the solution', to the machine which we also apply to ourselves. If they do the same things as us, perhaps they can show us how to explain what we do.

But, the objection goes, they don't do the same thing as us, or only within the range of the analogy between weak and strong action-attributions. They do something we can call 'computing' in a weak, observer-relative sense of this term; which relative to another observer might be described as 'mantric-clicking'. We do something we call 'computing' in the strong sense, not observer-relative. How can we be so sure that an underlying process describable by the weak sense explains the overt action described in the strong sense? These are after all, very different, distinguished by everything that divides things possessing the significance feature from things without it. 'Computing' engines present some analogies to computing people, but they offer as yet no hint of how one might account for this salient feature of the latter, that they are agents, and act. Indeed, it has been essential to their utility that we can understand and operate these machines without reference to the significance feature.

Those who are nevertheless sure of the machine paradigm must be grounding their confidence on the belief that we can somehow ignore the significance feature. Why? Well presumably because of the analogy I mentioned above with the misleading appearances which the progress of science has had to ignore. Cognitive psychologists are frequently dismissive of arguments of phenomenologists on the grounds that phenomenology can be very misleading as to underlying structure. The implication is that phenomenology gives us surface appearance, not anything about the nature of the explanandum.

The assumption underlying this dismissive attitude must be that the significance feature is a misleading surface appearance, like the movement of the sun, or perhaps a purely phenomenal one, like phenomenal colour or felt heat, to be set aside in any rigourous characterization of the events to be explained. This gets to seem a plausible view the more we repeat to ourselves that computing machines compute. The difference between computing and 'computing', between real and observer-relative performances, comes to seem a rather secondary matter. The significance feature comes to seem like a pure matter of the inner feel, something to do with the way the whole process is experienced from the inside, or perhaps at best, a tag of honour we accord to agents, that they bear their predicates non-relatively; but in no case an important defining feature of the explanandum.

But this, of course, is mad. There is all the difference in the world between a creature with and one without the significance feature. It is not just a detachable feature that action has in some medium of internal representation, but is essential to action itself. The supposedly secondary, dispensable character of the significance feature disappears once we cease to dwell on that small range of actions which have plausible machine analogues. Once we look to feelings, emotions, or actions which are defined in terms of them, or of moral categories, aesthetic categories, etc., like 'saving one's honour', 'telling the truth', etc., we run out of machine analogues to be bemused by.

Or, if we are still bemused, it is because we are in the grip of an old metaphysical view, one embedded in our epistemological tradition, which makes us see our awareness as an inner medium of representation, which monitors (partly and sometimes misleadingly) what goes on in our bodies and the world. This is the ghost of the old dualism, still stalking the battlements of its materialist successor-states.

Consciousness is primarily understood as representation[6]. As such it is separable from the processes which it monitors, or of which it is a symptom. If it plays any role in explaining these processes, it must be in interacting with them. Since interaction is ruled out on materialist assumptions, it cannot be allowed any explanatory role at all. It can only serve as a (possibly misleading) way of access to the processes which are the stuff of behavioural science.

On this view, the primary difference between us and machines is that we are clearly conscious and they don't seem to be. Even this latter isn't entirely sure, and cognitive theorists begin to hedge bets when they are dragged onto this terrain: perhaps after all one day machines will get sufficiently complex to have consciousness? And will we ever know?

The discussion here gets ragged and rather silly; a sign that we're on the wrong track. And so we are. For the crucial difference between men and machines is not consciousness, but rather the significance feature. We also enjoy consciousness, because we are capable of focusing on the significance things have for us, and above all of transforming them through formulation in language. That is not unimportant; but the essential thing that divides us from machines is what also separates our lesser cousins the dumb brutes from them, that things have significance for us non-relatively. This is the context in which alone something like consciousness is possible for us, since we achieve it by focusing on the significance of things, principally in language, and this is something we *do*.

The necessary distinction to understand the contrast between us and machines is not mental/physical, or inner/outer, but possessing/ not possessing the significance feature. Once we understand this, we can see that this feature can't be marginalized as though it concerned merely the way things *appear* to us, as though it were a feature merely of an inner medium of representation. On the contrary, it plays an absolutely crucial role in explaining what we do, and hence defines the kind of creatures we are.

We can see this best if we look again at our emotions, such as the example of shame above. As beings capable of shame, we experience certain emotions, and we react in certain ways to our situation and to each other. This is not just a fact of how things appear to us inside; this is a crucial fact about how we are and what we do. This is evident in the fact that in order to explain our behaviour, we have to use emotion terms like 'shame' and corresponding situation descriptions like 'humiliating'. In accounting for what we do, there is no substitute for a language which makes sense only as applied to beings with the significance feature, the language of shame, humiliation, pride, honour, dignity, love, admiration, etc. It's as fundamental as that.

In other words, when we say that the significance feature is essential to our self-understanding as agents, we are not saying that it is inseparable from our representations in an inner medium, whose deliverances are as dispensable to an explanation of behaviour as our perceptions of the sun in the sky are to our account of the solar system. We are rather saying, that once we understand ourselves as *agents*, rather than, say, as physical objects on all fours with others, including inanimate ones, we understand ourselves as beings of whom the significance feature is an essential character.

Once we see this, we have to stop treating it as matter of surface appearance, and the plausibility begins to dissipate that surrounds the notion that we can explain computing, and much else, by the 'computing' of machines.

But perhaps one more desperate measure is possible. Supposing we challenged our entire self-understanding as agents. Perhaps it is all systematically misleading. Perhaps the only way to explain what we do is to look at ourselves as machines, and explain what we do in the same terms.

This is a radical suggestion, and one which undercuts cognitive psychology from another direction. Its ambition is just to give an account in psychological terms, terms that apply peculiarly to human beings, and perhaps some animals, and that can be seen as developments or more rigorous variants of the terms we understand ourselves with in ordinary life. Cognitive psychology is looking for a relatively autonomous science of human behaviour. It would not be satisfied just with a science that entirely abandoned the psychological, and dealt with us simply in the language of physics, say.

But it is also a suggestion that does nothing to solve our problem. For we cannot abandon our understanding of ourselves as agents. This is bound up with our practice as agents. Self-understanding is constitutive, as we saw, of what we are, what we do, what we feel. Understanding ourselves as agents is not in the first place a theory, it is an essential part of our practice. It is inescapably involved in our functioning as human beings.

The significance feature is at the centre of human life, most palpably in that we come to understandings with the people about the significance of things. There is no relationship, from the most external and frosty to the most intimate and defining, which is not based on some understanding about the meanings things have for us. In the most important cases, of course, one of the things whose significance is understood between us is our relationship itself.

That is why the significance perspective is not an arbitrary one among human beings, one way of explaining how these organisms work among other possible ones. It is not even primarily a theoretical perspective on our behaviour. We couldn't function as human beings, that is as humans among other humans, for five minutes outside this perspective.[7]

In other words, we could have no relations at all if we didn't treat ourselves and others as agents.[8]

We can put this another way, and say that this self-understanding as agents is part of the reality it purports to understand. That is why a science of behaviour in terms of physics alone, even should such a thing prove possible, would still not answer the legitimate questions which psychology sets for itself: what is it that underlies and makes possible our functioning as agents, and the self-understanding that goes with it?

But, to sum up the objection announced at the start of this section, it isn't at all clear how the machine paradigm is going to help us with these questions either.

IV

But hold on. I don't think one can say flat out that the machine paradigm won't help us. Maybe it can produce some scientifically important results farther down the road. What can be said is that it isn't a whole lot more plausible than a number of other approaches; and that it only looks strongly plausible as long as you overlook the significance feature. And you only do that, I think, if you're still in the grip of the dualist metaphysic (even though transposed in a materialist key) which comes to us from the epistemological tradition.

Once you do see the importance of the significance feature, it is evident that computing machines can at best go some of the way to explaining human computation, let alone intelligent, adaptive performance generally. To be told that underlying my ball-catching are patterns of firing in the cortex analogous to those in electronic computers gives me as yet no idea of how these can help to account for (non-observer-relative) *action*, producing as they do a quite different kind of operation in the machine. What we have to discover is how processes analogous to machine computations could combine with others to produce real action, if this paradigm is to have a future. And this is no mean task. Indeed, no-one has the slightest idea how even to go about pursuing it. In this context, the glaring disanalogies between machines and human performance, e.g. the features discussed in the first section, can no longer be dismissed as mere appearances. They are rather major challenges to the very legitimacy of the paradigm.

Machine-modelled explanations of human performance, of the kind cognitive psychology offers, would have to relate to this performance understood as action in the role of an underlying explanation. We have this when phenomena on one level are explained by a theory invoking factors at another level, where this second level offers us the more basic explanation. An explanation in theory T is more basic than one in T', where the explanatory factors ultimate for T' are in turn explained in T.

We can clarify the predicament of cognitive psychology if we lay out three types of cases of such underlying explanation.

Case (1): The descriptions made and factors cited at the higher level turn out to be confused or mistaken when we achieve the deeper level explanation. In this case, we have not so much an explanation as an explaining away. An historical example of this is the distinction in Aristotelian cosmology between the supra-lunar and incorruptible, and the infra-lunar and corruptible. This was important to explain a whole host of things, including why the stars above go in perfect circles. The whole thing was just a mistake, and what survives is just *appearances* which can be explained in terms of the new cosmology; but the crucial distinctions of the old one turn out to be unfounded. We can now explain why things looked that way, but we know they aren't.

The higher level explanation is discredited, because the distinctions it draws don't in fact correspond to any genuine explanatory factors. The higher level operates with concepts and descriptions whereamong no explanatory factors are to be found. There never was a science here. Just as if I tried to explain the movements of the planets in terms of their colours in the telescope. I might note all sorts of patterns, but I should never in a million years be able to explain why they move as they do. For the relevant factors are mass and distance.

Case (2): Here we have a genuine explanation on the higher level, which is the object of a more basic explanation on the lower. As an example: we explain the wood disintegrating into ash by its being put in the fire. But we can give a deeper explanation in terms of the kinetic energy of the molecules. This is more basic, in that it accounts for the regularity by which we explained things at the higher level. With the kinetic theory, we understand the why of heat-transmission in general, and can see now why the same effect could be produced by a laser, for instance; why similar effects don't flow from heating metal, and so on.

The higher level explanation is genuine; in this, the case differs from (1). But it is dispensable. The higher explanation can always be eliminated in favour of the lower without loss. The latter not only gives us more, but covers all the same terrain as the former. There are no factors explanatory of heating/burning phenomena which are available on the higher level in such terms as 'fire', 'charring', etc., for which there are not correlates on the lower level, which can do the same explanatory job in the context of a more comprehensive theory. So for explaining heat, there is nothing we do with our phenomenal language which we couldn't do better in the kinetic-theory language. The phenomenal language is indispensable to describe how things are for us in our everyday identification of things; we need them to identify things as they figure in our perceptions, but otherwise, for the purpose of scientific characterization of the domain, not at all.

Case (3): Here there is also a valid higher level explanation. And there is also a theory of underlying structures which helps us explain how things happen as they do, and gives us some of the conditions of the higher level events occurring as they do. But unlike case (2), we cannot dispense with the higher level descriptions for the purpose of explaining the phenomena of the domain concerned. Some of the crucial explanatory factors are only available at this level; or to put it negatively, they can't all be identified at the lower level. To seek them all there would be as fruitless as seeking the factors explaining planetary orbits in their colours.

I don't have an incontestable example. Let me just offer one which is relative to our explanatory resources at the present time, without prejudging whether we will take things beyond this in the future or not. A fleet assembles for war. This is a pattern of ship-movements. At what corresponds to the more basic level, these can be explained in terms of the operations of engines, pistons, screws, etc. This level is essential if we are to get an explanatory handle on some of the features of this pattern. For instance, it is indispensable to explain why in some cases, ships stopped and began to be tossed by the sea (cases of engine failure), why some ships went faster than others, why some took a circuitous route (e.g., to get more fuel); and so on.

But if you want to understand why they are steaming towards this pattern, you have to be told that war has been declared, and that they are forming the fleet for such and such an offensive action. You need to have recourse here to the 'highest level' language of policy and politico-military goals and intentions. If you remain on the lower, engine-room level, you'll never identify the crucial factors, in the same way as the factors behind planetary motion couldn't be found in colour discourse.

I repeat that this example is relative to our present explanatory resources. It is not meant to *prove* that we couldn't discover one day some explanation on a neurophysiological level which would render our policy- and intention-descriptions dispensable. I am just trying to give a picture of a third possible case, which *may* turn out to have instances at the end of the day. Because, though no-one can say that such a neurophysiological language of explanation is impossible, there is even less ground for assuring us that it must be there to be found. Case (3) may yet turn out to be the model for deeper level explanations of human behaviour. My hunch is that it will.

But forget my hunches. The point of this was to provide a typology in which to understand the possible relations of underlying explanations to our action account.

It's clear that case (1) has no application here. To say that it's analogous to the infra-/supra-lunar distinction amounts to saying that our classifications of events as actions are wholly illusory. But since the self-understanding of ourselves as agents is essential to our acting, this is a claim which must remain meaningless and preposterous to us. Really to see the distinction between action and non-action as like the infra-/supra-lunar one would be to be incapable of acting. This is not an alternative we need consider.

There remain (2) and (3). The assumption of cognitive psychologists seems to me to be that case (2) offers the appropriate model. The underlying explanation, in a language appropriate to computing machines, gives us all the explanatory factors; the action account presents things as they look to us. The model here would be the kinetic theory in relation to a phenomenal account of heating and heat transmission.

But I have argued above that this claim is prematurely made. Certainly the machine paradigm at present doesn't offer any hint how we could hope to discover all the explanatory factors in its terms. In particular, we haven't the foggiest idea how it might help us to account for the significance feature of agents. If we ever do manage to account for the significance feature in mechanistic terms, then we will indeed have instantiated case (2). But until that day – should it ever come – case (3) has got to figure as a very plausible contestant.

For in fact, that's where we are now. Underlying explanations especially neurophysiological, can offer us more basic explanations of some important phenomena: of certain features of development, of differential capacities, of breakdowns, and a host of other matters. But to explain fully motivated behaviour, we need an account of what is happening in terms of action, desires, goals, aspirations. We have no metaphysical guarantee that after an immense series of discoveries, refinements, and breakthroughs, the basic structure of our explanations of ourselves will not still be the same: a variant of case (3). What purport to be assurances to the contrary are based on the illusions of traditional dualism.

On one reading of the term, case (2) can be called a case of reduction of the higher to the lower level. (In a more denigrating sense, we sometimes reserve 'reduction' for cases of (1).) On this reading, it looks as though I am classing cognitive psychologists as proponents of reduction, more particularly, reduction of psychology to some underlying explanation. But this they (or many of them) claim not to be.

We have only to look at Fodor's book.[9] In his first chapter, he defends the independence and viability of the psychological enterprise against both behaviourism and physicalistic reductivism. A reductivist relationship holds, Fodor argues, between a special science (like, e.g., psychology) and a more general one (like physics), when the laws of the former can be linked to laws of the latter via correlation statements which are themselves law-like. The crucial feature of this relationship would be that the natural kind terms of the special science, those in which its laws could be formulated, would be type-identical with the natural kind terms of the general science, i.e., physics.

Fodor's characterization of reduction resembles case (2) above, in that the special science is dispensable – although perhaps he makes the requirement a bit too stringent in demanding that the correlations all be law-like.

Now Fodor thinks that this kind of reductive relation is very unlikely to hold between the sciences of man and physics. He takes an example from economics: Gresham's Law. It is surely extremely unlikely that all cases of monetary exchange of which Gresham's Law holds, i.e. where monies of different quality are in circulation, should all fall under the same physical description; or otherwise put, that the physical description of all such cases should exhibit a natural kind in physics. 'Banal considerations suggest that a physical description which covers all such events must be wildly disjunctive.'[10] Even if one should manage, at the moment when human society was about to go under, to survey all previous cases of monetary exchange, and find some vast baggy disjunction under which all these cases fit in physical terms, this would still fail to be a law; because it would not necessarily help at all in counter-factual cases. We would not be able to conclude that, if the universe had gone on for another year, the physical conformation of the monetary exchanges in it would have been such and so.[11]

But, Fodor argues, we don't need to espouse type-type identities in order to save materialism, science, etc. It is sufficient to embrace what he calls 'token physicalism': 'the claim that all the events that the sciences talk about are physical events'.[12] This is compatible with the type of event that a special science picks out (like monetary exchange) being realized physically in an indefinite number of ways – so long as it is always realized physically.

Espousing token physicalism, and rejecting type-type identities, allows for the special sciences deploying concepts which are unsubstitutable. The special sciences need these if they are to 'state such true, counter-factual supporting generalisations as there are to state'.[13] For if the natural kind terms of a special science only correlate with loose, open disjunctions in another science, then we can't state the laws explanatory of the events that the special science deals with in the other science. For to explain, to give an account of what happens, is to license counter-factuals; and open disjunctions by definition license no counter-factuals. The natural kind terms of our special science are in this case unsubstitutable.

Another science may cast a great deal of light on the underpinnings of these natural kinds. In particular, it may lay bare important conditions of their functioning as they do; so that the other science may give us explanations of exceptions and breakdowns. But it cannot substitute for the special science; and in this sense, we can see the natural kinds this latter science designates as part of the furniture of things.

Fodor's description of the status of a special science like psychology fits my case (3). The special science is indispensable, because the crucial explanatory factors (read, natural kinds) are only discoverable on the level of this special science; on the lower level they are not identifiable. Just as, for example, the class of planets of a given mass form an indefinitely open disjunction described in colour terms, so do the cases of monetary exchange in physical terms.

But then surely I am wrong to tax cognitivists with reductionism, with taking case (2) as their model?

No, I'm not. First, because we're not talking about the same things. When Fodor talks of the relation of psychology to physics, he's not talking about our account of ourselves as agents. His 'psychology' is an account of what we do in computational terms, and the reductive issue for him arises between an account at this level and one at the physical or neurological level. He is quite oblivious of the difference between an account in computational terms and one which characterizes us as agents with the significance feature.

Indeed, Fodor's thesis of the irreducibility of psychology emerges originally from a reflection on computing machines. It was the recognition that two machines might be the same in the programme run on them, and yet be very different in their physical structures and principles, which gave rise to the notion that an account of what they do in computational terms could not correlate with general laws on a physical level.

This was the basis of the thesis known as 'functionalism' in psychology. But this was because it was simply taken for granted that a 'psychological' account of what we do would be a computational one analogous to those we apply to machines. Fodor clearly makes this identification. Part of his argument against reductionism assumes it.

Even if there are neurological kinds co-extensive with psychological kinds as things stand now, he argues, the correlations cannot be lawful. 'For it seems increasingly likely that there are nomologically possible systems other than organisms (viz. automata) which satisfy the kind predicates of psychology but which satisfy no neurological predicates at all.'[14]

The 'psychology' here is obviously not what I am talking about. What we normally understand as the predicates of psychology, those which involve the significance feature, plainly don't apply to machines. Nor have we anything but the vaguest fantasies as to how they might apply to machines we design in the future. The 'kind predicates' of psychology which we might think it 'increasingly likely' that automata will satisfy are computational performance terms applied in their weak, observer-relative sense.

The psychology whose irreducibility Fodor is defending is one which is just as much a science of computing machines as of humans. It has nothing to do with our account of ourselves as agents. The difference between these he just ignores, most likely for some of the reasons discussed above, owing to the baleful influence of traditional dualism. So whatever the relation between the computational and physical levels, Fodor plainly construes that between the computational account and the one in terms of agency in a reductive way, on the model of cases (1) or (2).

Secondly, it is not so clear after all that Fodor really can carry through his account of the psychology–physics relation as a case (3). If a paradigm of this relation is to be found in computing machines, whose programme can be matched by machines of different design, then it is not so clear that counter-factuals can't be found at the more basic level.

For any given (physical) type of machine, there are no counter-factuals on the computational level that can't be matched, and explained by counter-factuals at the engineering level. Counter-factuals like 'if the programme had been changed in such and such a way, then . . .', or 'if the problem had been posed in such and such a way, then . . .' can be given a deeper level explanation in terms of the way the machine is wired, connected up, or whatever. If this were not the case, we wouldn't be able to build, design, improve, etc. such machines.

Of course, other machines can be constructed on other principles, such that the deeper level explanations would invoke quite different factors. One machine, let's say, operates electronically; the other is run by fuel and has gears. The underlying accounts will be very different. And there may be an indefinite number of such machines which we might design to run the same types of programme.

This certainly shows that the level of programme design is in some way essential to us, that we couldn't go about doing what we do if we were to abandon this level of discourse. But we couldn't go so far as to say that the crucial explanatory factors are unavailable on the lower level.

Contrast what seems plausible with the Gresham's Law example. It is not just that one case of monetary exchange with media of different quality will involve gold and silver, the next gold and bronze, the next dollars and deutschmarks, the next old and new currency, etc. Even in a given case, you can't match counter-factuals on the economics level with those on the physical level. 'If people come to believe that the king is no longer adulterating the silver coinage, then gold will come back into circulation' corresponds to no counter-factual on the level of bodily movement, say, even if we restrict our attention to this context. People can come to believe this in all sorts of ways; they can be told in French or English, or in sign language; they can come across silver coins newly minted, that seem heavier; they can deduce it from the behaviour of merchants; and so on indefinitely.

We might complain that this comparison is unfair, that we have to draw the boundaries of a context narrower in the Gresham's Law case. But this just makes the difference more palpable. We don't know how to draw such boundaries in the monetary exchange case so as to make for stable relations of deeper level explanation. The ever-present possibility of original speech acts which inaugurate new extensions of meaning makes this impossible.

By contrast, in the domain of computing machines, there are such stable relations of more basic explanation in each context; and the boundaries between the contexts are clearly and unambiguously demarcated by the (physical) type of machine. We are never at a loss for lower-level counter-factuals to explain our higher-level ones. True, there are an indefinite number of such possible contexts of computation. But they are each clearly demarcated, and within each one the relation between levels of explanation conforms to case (2). The absence of match between natural kind terms at the two levels of discourse can itself be explained in terms of a difference between natural kinds, viz., the types of machine.

This suggests that we ought to distinguish two questions: a) do the laws and licensed counter-factuals have the same scope on the two levels? and b) are there laws and licensed counter-factuals at all on the lower level? The answer to b) may be affirmative, even while that to a) is negative. In this case, it is not unambiguously true that reductive relations don't hold. This is the kind of case where we want to speak of systems which are analogous but not homologous. For each homologous class of machines, however, the reduction is a perfect case (2), and if this were the only domain we had to consider, it would never occur to us to question a reductivist construal.

But in a genuine case (3), the answer to b) is negative, and this is a quite different predicament.

Fodor seems to have elided what I have called case (3) and what I might call a multi-contexted case (2); and this may be connected with his having elided the two issues: the reduction of computational psychology to physics, and the reduction of our action understanding to computational psychology: or rather, his having invisibly subsumed the second question in the first. Because the second does seem to call for a case (3) solution, while the first seems to conform to this special kind of multiplex case (2).

But this is all part of his ignoring the issue around the significance feature, which amounts, I have tried to show, to a reductionism of a very strong kind.

V

I have tried to draw a map in the preceding pages of the disputed terrain around cognitive psychology. As I acknowledged at the outset, this map is far from neutral. This is in the nature of things. It is the property of this kind of profound philosophical dispute that the two sides differ even in their maps of the contested zone. For one general staff, the redoubt 'reduction' is seen as clearly outside their perimeter, an undefended position now reduced to any empty shell enclosing rubble; for their opponents, it is the centre work of the enemy line. For one side, the regiments of phenomenological artillery are seen as harmless noisemakers, their shells bursting without effect far off the target; for the opponents, their cumulative effect is devastating, rendering the enemy line ultimately untenable before a determined charge of changing the subject.

My central claim has been that the two sides ultimately confront each other around the issue of the significance of significance. Does it really matter that things matter? For one view, the significance feature is treated as having merely to do with the way things appear to us. It can thus be sidelined when it comes to the serious business of explaining our performance. On the other view, this sidelining is an evasion. The significance feature is crucial to the explanandum in the sciences of man; and if we consult our best explanatory practice so far, it seems ineradicable from the explanans.

It is this difference of view which underlies the multiple cross-purposes which bedevil the debate, the lack of fit of the two maps of the combat zone. We can only resolve the cross-purposes, I want to claim, by explicitly raising the issue of the significance of significance. Once we do, there is in my opinion little doubt whose map turns out to be the more inaccurate: it is the Enlightenment army which has badly misconceived the shape of the terrain. They have not strengthened their line as they thought, but remain in partial occupation of the porous earthworks of positivism; and they are not at all deployed to defend these against their enemy's most devastating attack. They are just fortunate that in the perverse conditions of philosophical warfare such disarray is not inevitably followed by defeat.

Bibliography

Adorno, Theodor W., *Negative Dialektik* (1973); translated as *Negative Dialectics* (1973).

Anderson, J.R., *Language, Memory, and Thought* (1976).

Apel, K.O., *Analytic Philosophy of Language and the Geisteswissenschaften* (1967).

Austin, J.L., 'A Plea for Excuses', in *Philosophical Papers* (1961).

Ayer, A.J., *Language, Truth and Logic* (1969).

Barnes, J., 'Aristote chez les Anglophones', *Critique*, 100 (1980).

Bennett, J., *Kant's Analytic* (1963).

——, *Kant's Dialectic* (1968).

Boden, Margaret, *Artificial Intelligence and Natural Man* (1977).

Cavell, Stanley, *Must We Mean What We Say?* (1976).

Chomsky, Noam, *Language and Mind* (1968).

——, *Rules and Representations* (1980).

Cohen, G.A., *Marx's Theory of History: A Defence* (1978).

Davidson, D., 'Truth and Meaning', *Synthese*, 17 (1974).

——, 'Reply to Foster', in Evans and McDowell (eds.), *Truth and Meaning* (1976).

Dennett, Daniel, *Brainstorms* (1978).

Derrida, J., *De la grammatologie* (1967); translated as *Of Grammatology* (1977).

——, *L'Écriture et la différence* (1967); translated as *Writing and Difference* (1978).

——, 'La structure, le signe et le jeu dans le discours des sciences humaines', in *L'Écriture et la différence;* translated as 'Structure, Sign, and Play in the Discourse of the Human Sciences', in *Writing and Difference*.

——, *La Dissémination* (1972); translated as *Dissemination* (1981).

——, 'La mythologie blanche', in *Marges de la philosophie* (1972); translated as 'White Mythology: Metaphor in the Text of Philosophy', *New Literary History*, 6 (1974).

——, 'Positions', in *Positions* (1972; translated 1981); translated as 'Positions', *Diacritics*, 2 & 3 (1972/73).

——, *Éperons: Les styles des Nietzsche* (1976).

Douglas, Mary, *Rules and Meanings* (1973).

Dreyfus, Hubert, *What Computers Can't Do* (1979).

Dummett, M., 'Wittgenstein's Philosophy of Mathematics', *The Philosophical Review*, 67 (1958).

——, *Frege: Philosophy of Language* (1973).

——, 'What is a Theory of Meaning?', in Guttenplan (ed.), *Mind and Language* (1975).

——, 'Can Analytical Philosophy be Systematic, and Ought it to Be?', in *Truth and Other Enigmas* (1979).

Fodor, J., *The Language of Thought* (1975).

Foucault, M., *Discipline and Punish* (1977).

——, *The History of Sexuality*, Vol. 1 (1978).

Frege, G., 'The Thought: A Logical Inquiry', in Strawson (ed.), *Philosophical Logic* (1967).

——, 'Logik', in *Nachgelassene Schriften* (1969).

Gadamer, H.G., *Truth and Method* (1975).

Geertz, C., *The Interpretation of Cultures* (1973).

Habermas, J., *Zur Logik der Sozialwissenschaften* (1970).

——, *Erkenntnis und Interesse* (1973); translated as *Knowledge and Human Interests* (1978).

——, *Communication and the Evolution of Society* (1979).

Hare, R., 'Philosophical Discoveries', in Rorty (ed.), *The Linguistic Turn* (1967).

Hegel, G.W.F., *Logik*, in *Werke in zwanzig Bänden*, 8 (1970); translated as *Hegel's Logic* (1975).

Heidegger, M., *Being and Time* (1962).

Horkheimer, Max, 'Traditionelle und Kritische Theorie', in *Kritische Theorie*, 2 (1968); translated as 'Traditional and Critical Theory', in Connerton (ed.), *Critical Sociology* (1976).

Kuhn, T.S., *The Structure of Scientific Revolutions* (1970).

Mackay, D.M., 'The Mind's Eye View of the Brain', in Pribram (ed.), *Brain and Behaviour 4, Adaptation* (1977).

Mackie, J.L., *Truth, Probability and Paradox* (1972).

McDowell, J., 'On the Sense and Reference of a Proper Name', *Mind*, 87 (1978).

Mead, G.H., *Mind, Self, and Society* (1934).

Merleau-Ponty, M., *The Phenomenology of Perception* (1962).

——, *Signs* (1964).

——, *The Prose of the World* (1973).

Newell, A. and H. Simon, *Human Problem Solving* (1972).

Putnam, H., ' "Si dieu est mort, alors tout est permis . . .": Réflexions sur la philosophie du langage', *Critique*, 100 (1980).

Quine, W.V.O., *Word and Object* (1960).

——, 'Epistemology Naturalized' and 'Ontological Relativity', in *Ontological Relativity and Other Essays* (1969).

——, 'Methodological Reflections on Current Linguistic Theory', in Davidson and Harman (eds.), *Semantics of Natural Languages* (1972).

Rorty, R., *Philosophy and the Mirror of Nature* (1980).

Russell, B., 'Philosophy of Logical Atomism', *Monist*, 28 & 29 (1918/19).

——, *The Philosophy of Leibniz* (1937).

Ryle, G., 'Systematically Misleading Expressions', in *Collected Papers*, Vol. 2 (1968).

Saussure, F., *Course in General Linguistics* (1966).

Schlesinger, G., *Method in the Physical Sciences* (1963).

Schutz, A., 'Concept and Theory Formation in the Social Sciences', in Dallmayr and McCarthy (eds.), *Understanding and Social Inquiry* (1977).

Searle, J., *Speech Acts* (1969).

——, 'Minds, Brains, and Programmes', in *The Behavioural and Brain Sciences* (1980).

Simon, H., 'The Architecture of Complexity', in *The Science of the Artificial* (1969).

——, *Models of Discovery* (1977).

Sloman, A., *The Computer Revolution in Philosophy* (1978).

Strawson, P.F., *Individuals* (1959).

——, *The Bounds of Sense* (1966).

——, 'Freedom and Resentment', in *Freedom and Resentment and Other Essays* (1974).

Stroud, B., *Hume* (1972).

Wiener, N., *Cybernetics* (1961).

Winch, P., *The Idea of a Social Science and its Relation to Philosophy* (1958).

Wittgenstein, L., *Philosophical Investigations* (1953).

——, *Remarks on the Foundations of Mathematics* (1956).

——, *Blue and Brown Books* (1958).

——, *Tractatus Logico-Philosophicus* (1961).

——, 'Bemerkungen über Frazers *The Golden Bough*', *Synthese*, 17 (1967); translated in *The Human World*, May 1971, pp. 18–41.

——, *Lectures and Conversations on Aesthetics, Psychology, and Religious Belief* (1967).

——, *Zettel* (1967).

Notes

The Role of Philosophy in the Human Sciences

1 I would like to thank A.J. Ayer, Carol Ann Bernheim, the editors, David Wiggins and above all Peter Lipton for criticisms of an earlier draft of this paper and for extensive discussions.

Creation and Discovery: Wittgenstein on Conceptual Change

1 I employ the following standard abbreviations when referring to Wittgenstein's works: *RFM* = *Remarks on the Foundations of Mathematics*; *PI* = *Philosophical Investigations*. Roman numerals refer to the relevant Parts, arabic numerals to the relevant Sections.

2 This argument does not, of course, establish that it is wrong to treat *truth* as a property of sentences; only necessity is at stake here. Throughout the essay, I apply truth to both sentences and what sentences express.

3 See, for example, Michael Dummett's influential 'Wittgenstein's Philosophy of Mathematics'.

Post-Structuralism, Empiricism and Interpretation

1 Cf. Strawson, *The Bounds of Sense* (on Kant's *Critique of Pure Reason*); Barry Stroud, *Hume*; G.A. Cohen, *Marx's Theory of History: A Defence*; Jonathan Bennett, *Kant's Analytic* and *Kant's Dialectic*; and even Michael Dummett's *Frege: Philosophy of Language* (which does much to 'update' Frege).

2 Derrida has published numerous articles devoted to literary texts, or to the literary criticism of philosophical texts. Few of these have been translated. The more important are: 'From Restricted to General Economy: A Hegelianism without Reserve' (in *Writing and Difference*); 'La Double Séance' and 'La Dissémination' (both in *Dissemination*); and *Éperons* (published in a French/English version).

3 Michael Dummett, 'What is a Theory of Meaning?'; Donald Davidson,

'Truth and Meaning'; John McDowell, 'On the Sense and Reference of a Proper Name'.

[4] About this relation Derrida says: 'Strangely enough, this comes down to treating every signifier as a metaphor for the signified, while the classical concept of metaphor denotes only the substitution of one signified for another so that one becomes the signifier for the other' ('White Mythology', p. 27).

[5] I would like to thank everyone associated with The Camargo Foundation, in Cassis, France, for their support and hospitality while this paper was being written. The afternoon indigo of the Mediterranean offered welcome relief from the long nights spent with Messrs. Derrida, Quine, and Co.

Critical Theory: Between Ideology and Philosophy

[1] My thanks for comments are due to Tim Mitchell and Ted Schatzki.

[2] Quotations follow the English translation cited with slight modifications, except for quotations from Adorno which are my own.

The Prescription is Description: Wittgenstein's View of the Human Sciences

[1] Wittgenstein's philosophical work is often divided into two distinct philosophies – an earlier, represented by the *Tractatus Logico-Philosophicus* (1921), and a later, represented by the *Philosophical Investigations* (1953 – written in the forties). Here I am concerned with the views of the later philosophy and say nothing about the relations between the two phases.

[2] See P. Winch, *The Idea of a Social Science and its Relation to Philosophy*, and K.O. Apel, *Analytic Philosophy of Language and the Geisteswissenschaften*. Winch's views are briefly discussed in note 7, but there is no space to discuss Apel.

[3] Abbreviations to Wittgenstein's works used in this paper are as follows: *BB* = *Blue and Brown Books*; *LC* = *Lectures and Conversations on Aesthetics, Psychology, and Religious Belief*; *PI* = *Philosophical Investigations*; *RFG* = 'Bemerkungen über Frazers *The Golden Bough*' (page references to German and English versions have been listed); *RFM* = *Remarks on the Foundations of Mathematics*; *Z* = *Zettel*.

[4] Wittgenstein is unclear about whether all philosophical questions other than questions of essence fall in the class of questions he calls 'illegitimate'. This is especially true of ethical and political questions. His targets in much of his discussion of philosophy are the great 'metaphysical' questions of the history of philosophy (he sometimes speaks not of the philosopher but of the metaphysician). But he never clarifies which problems are metaphysical.

⁵ *PI* 371 and 373 show clearly that Wittgenstein thought that his method can answer questions of essence. Hence he could not have considered such questions themselves, only the theoretical attempts to answer them, illegitimate.

⁶ Wittgenstein's idea of conceptual elucidation is thus very different from the notion of conceptual analysis utilized in twentieth-century analytical philosophy. The latter proceeds by separating concepts into their components, or by giving necessary and sufficient conditions for their application. Wittgenstein believes that there are no such components or conditions (one cannot define the set of all possible instances of a given concept); practical understanding cannot be transcribed into a set of rules.

⁷ At this point it might be appropriate to mention Winch's interpretation of Wittgenstein's views about the type of understanding sought by such sciences. At the foundation of his interpretation lies a misunderstanding of Wittgenstein's discussion of rules. Winch claims that Wittgenstein argues that it is actors' implicit understanding of the rules governing their behaviour that enables them to act in ways intelligible to each other. Thus the type of rule that he attributes to Wittgenstein lies somewhere between the two kinds of rules I discussed. It is like the rules an expression of which is involved in action, in that it is an actor's cognizance of a rule that determines that he acts in a way that counts as an application of it; and it is like the rules which describe regularities in that there is no conscious cognizance of them. Winch then goes on to conclude that the understanding of actions and practices sought by interpretative human science involves the discovery of the rules that govern them. According to Winch, this requires that the investigator become a participant in the practice he attempts to understand.

Besides the confusion about rules, this interpretation is inadequate because Winch nowhere discusses the notions of description and perspicuous representation (it is only fair to mention that Winch's book was published before Wittgenstein's remarks on Frazer appeared). Winch is right, however, in emphasizing that participation in, or rather interaction with, the practices one studies, whenever possible, is an important element in coming to understand them. I disagree with Winch, however, if he thinks that Wittgenstein believes that interaction is necessary in order to achieve understanding. Wittgenstein advocates the same method for history, where interaction is not possible, as for social anthropology. So, in the latter field, it must be at least theoretically possible to give descriptions of one's subjects without interacting with them and yet still achieve the desired everyday understanding of them. For all intents and purposes, however, one needs such interaction. This is especially true if the investigator does not understand the language spoken by his subjects; though even here, according to Wittgenstein, it is theoretically possible to understand what they say without communicating with them. Success at interacting on an everyday level with one's subjects is also the only *test* of whether one has achieved an everyday understanding of them.

8   This description of action agrees with the descriptions given by the early Heidegger and Merleau-Ponty. It is also illuminating to compare it with Mead's formulations. CF. M. Heidegger, *Being and Time*, pp. 95–122, 182–95; G.H. Mead, *Mind, Self, and Society*; M. Merleau-Ponty, *The Phenomenology of Perception*, especially Chapter 6; *The Prose of the World*, first few essays; and *Signs*, first few essays on language.

9   M. Foucault seems to have arrived at similar conclusions in his recent work. Cf, *Discipline and Punish*, and *The History of Sexuality, Vol. 1*.

10 The process of elaboration has already begun. In addition to the works by Heidegger, Merleau-Ponty, and Foucault cited above, consult: H.G. Gadamer, *Truth and Method*; C. Geertz, *The Interpretation of Cultures*; J. Habermas, *Zur Logik der Sozialwissenschaften*.

11 I am indebted to Hans Sluga and Michael Rosen for comments on earlier drafts of this paper. Without their persistent questions and complaints, it certainly would not have arrived at its current state. I would also like to thank Hubert Dreyfus who started me thinking about types of understanding.

The Significance of Significance: The Case of Cognitive Psychology

1   E.g. D. Dennett, *Brainstorms*; J. Fodor, *The Language of Thought*; M. Boden, *Artificial Intelligence and Natural Men*; A. Sloman, *The Computer Revolution in Philosophy*.

2   Cf. H. Dreyfus, *What Computers Can't Do*; J. Searle, 'Minds, Brains, and Programmes'. *The Behavioural and Brain Sciences*, 1980, 3, 417-57.

3   Cf. J. Fodor, op. cit., p. 73.

4   Loc. cit., emphasis added.

5   For cogent objections, see Dreyfus, op. cit.

6   Foucault has shown – if that's the term – how central this notion of representation is to the modern epistemological tradition.

7   I think this is what emerges from the very interesting analysis of Peter Strawson in his 'Freedom and Resentment' paper.

8   But by this, I don't mean that we necessarily treat them ethically, or as ends in themselves. Even our exploitative behaviour in the vast majority of cases takes our victims as agents. It can be argued, however, that there is a profound connection between our status as agents and the validity of such moral precepts as those of Kant.

9   Op. cit.

10 Op. cit. p. 15.

[11] Op. cit. p. 16.
[12] Op. cit. p. 12.
[13] Op. cit. p. 25.
[14] Op. cit. pp. 17–18.

Index